AUTHORITARIANISM

TRI◍S

*Each TRIOS book
addresses an important
theme in critical theory,
philosophy, or cultural
studies through three
extended essays written
in close collaboration by
leading scholars.*

AUTHORITARIANISM

THREE INQUIRIES
IN CRITICAL THEORY

WENDY
Brown

PETER E.
Gordon

MAX
Pensky

The University of Chicago Press
Chicago and London

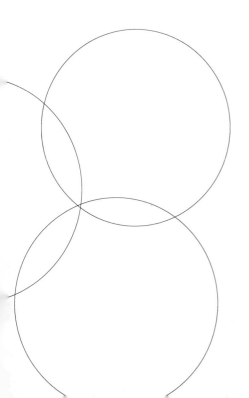

The University of Chicago Press, Chicago 60637
The University of Chicago Press, Ltd., London
© 2018 by The University of Chicago
All rights reserved. No part of this book may be used or reproduced in any manner
whatsoever without written permission, except in the case of brief quotations in critical
articles and reviews. For more information, contact the University of Chicago Press,
1427 E. 60th St., Chicago, IL 60637.
Published 2018
Printed in the United States of America

27 26 25 24 23 22 21 20 19   2 3 4 5

ISBN-13: 978-0-226-59713-3 (cloth)
ISBN-13: 978-0-226-59727-0 (paper)
ISBN-13: 978-0-226-59730-0 (e-book)
DOI: https://doi.org/10.7208/chicago/9780226597300.001.0001

Library of Congress Cataloging-in-Publication Data

Names: Brown, Wendy, 1955– author. | Gordon, Peter Eli, author. | Pensky, Max, 1961–
  author.
Title: Authoritarianism : three inquiries in critical theory / Wendy Brown, Peter E.
  Gordon, Max Pensky.
Other titles: Trios (Chicago, Ill.)
Description: Chicago ; London : The University of Chicago Press, 2018. | Series: Trios
Identifiers: LCCN 2018023746 | ISBN 9780226597133 (cloth : alk. paper) | ISBN
  9780226597270 (pbk. : alk. paper) | ISBN 9780226597300 (e-book)
Subjects: LCSH: Authoritarianism. | Democracy. | Liberalism.
Classification: LCC JC480 .B769 2018 | DDC 321.9—dc23
LC record available at https://lccn.loc.gov/2018023746

♾ This paper meets the requirements of ANSI/NISO Z39.48-1992 (Permanence of Paper).

CONTENTS

INTRODUCTION

CRITICAL THEORY IN AN
AUTHORITARIAN AGE

Wendy Brown,
Peter E. Gordon, and
Max Pensky

The current amazement that the things we are experiencing
are "still" possible in the twentieth century is *not* philosophical.

WALTER BENJAMIN

Liberal democracy today is in crisis, or, more accurately, in a state
of siege. Not only in the United States but in much of Europe and
in many nations across the globe, we are witnessing the advent
of a new era of antidemocratic politics, much of it with increasingly authoritarian features. In one country after another, social
movements and political leaders have succeeded in activating
reactionary populism, nativism, racism, and xenophobia. Rhet-
orics and policies of exclusion and marginalization of selected
groups have taken on a virulence and menace that would have
been intolerable in national politics not that many years ago,
violating implicit taboos that postwar democracies, in Western
Europe in particular, had incorporated as important parts of their
national political cultures. Hatred and resentment directed at
immigrants are expressed openly and violently, both by opportunistic political leaders and by citizens. Right-wing political

movements are emboldened to demand policies that permit, or even encourage, the undermining of constitutionalism and the rule of law. The growing presence and legitimacy of these movements brings a rising risk of antidemocratic political leadership, and the erosion of core elements of liberal democractic societies—egalitarianism, pluralism, and a free press—that had long seemed more stable and durable than they now appear.

These movements are increasingly difficult to explain, or explain away, in terms of the normal spectrum of electoral politics in liberal democratic states. There is a growing awareness—and anxiety—that they no longer fit within the received categories of political analysis: they challenge both conventional assumptions concerning the variability of democratic political forms and our historical terms for antidemocratic challenges. It is not clear even what terminology we should bring to analyzing and apprehending them. Authoritarian? Fascist? Populist? "Neo" versions of these?

Beyond the question of terminology there is uncertainty as to whether scholars of politics possess the tools and methods needed to analyze this crisis of democracy in the Euro-Atlantic world. If these movements pose a challenge to theoretical understanding, the difficulty is due in part to their appearance of historical novelty, but also in part to their seeming lack of ideological coherence. They are not all alike. Many appeal to an imaginary of ethnonational homogeneity secured by a strong and isolationist state animated by ferocious moral purpose, yet they graft these images of statism and nationalism to dogmas of neoliberal freedom that treat the state as freedom's greatest enemy. They aim to recapture a national sovereignty, ever more diminished by global powers and interconnectedness, and call for economic protectionism for the sake of "native" labor, yet at the same time they condemn regulated markets and policies of public provision (from education to health care) that promise even the most modest protection from capitalism's extreme inequalities, dislocations, and threats to planetary and species existence. These new political movements are, moreover, anti-political: they tend to denounce whatever goes by the name of conventional politics—its processes, compromises, institutions, and deliberative spaces. They are impatient with facts and with systematic analysis. Anger, resentment, denunciation, and a sense of frustration with lost entitlement all tend to close down the space for genuine insight and understanding, leaving the political sphere ripe for exploitation and mobilization by charismatic leaders.

*
**

The three essays collected in this volume draw on broad currents of critical theory to apprehend some dimensions of the current political crisis. In distinction from some other families of social and political theory, critical theory brings to the problem of the democratic crisis approaches that promise to study the intricate connections between subjective attitudes and large-scale historical trajectories, especially those of capitalism and the changing nature of states and social formations. The name "critical theory" derives from a distinctive moment in the history of modern social thought when a group of theorists in Frankfurt, Germany, were struggling to comprehend the failure of European democracies to oppose the slide into fascism in the 1930s. The Frankfurt School of critical theory began with a series of empirical research projects and theoretical hypotheses about the emergence and shape of authoritarian politics in that era. Drawing from, while revising, Western Marxism, Weberianism, and psychoanalysis, they developed a sophisticated repertoire of theoretical and empirical instruments by which to explain the new political situation. From their American exile in the 1940s, Max Horkheimer and Theodor W. Adorno collaborated with a range of American colleagues, most notably on *The Authoritarian Personality* (1950), but also on a host of lesser-known empirical studies attempting to assess and interpret the attitudinal changes and features that might have provided favorable conditions for the success of fascist or authoritarian political movements. In the years after the war, Herbert Marcuse published a series of widely read studies that employed elements of psychoanalytic theory to explain the social-psychological mechanisms at work in new, inconspicuous forms of social domination, in which resistant or transgressive impulses by the dominated are themselves harnessed to deepen social control.

Notwithstanding the very real differences between the fascist movements of the mid-twentieth century and the antidemocratic movements of our own time, critical theory remains of urgent relevance today, when many of the same phenomena that first aroused the critical attention of the Frankfurt School seem to have resurfaced in a new guise. To provide an elaborate listing of the continuities between past and present would be misleading, since the social and cultural forms have changed, in many cases dramatically so. But it is one of the real advantages of critical theory that it did not confine itself only to the diagnosis of its own present. In much of its empirical and theoretical work, it articulated latent social and cultural pathologies that had yet to reach their full potential. The founding critical theorists insisted that fascism does not mark a radical break from mass democracy but rather emerges as an intensification of its inner pathologies. More specifically, they argued that capitalist systems of production and consumption do not leave intact the "real" interests of democratic citizens who imagine that the mechanisms of representative democracy permit them to express their preferences through the procedure of elections. We cannot speak about the expression of genuine preferences in liberal democratic systems when a rich array of sociocultural norms shapes these preferences in advance. If this was the case when nativist movements reared their heads in the United States in the 1940s, it is all the more true today, when the logic of neoliberalism has extended its reach into all domains of life.

Critical theory has also expanded its reach beyond the confines of the original Frankfurt School, and as we conceive it today, may permit us to extend and modify the insights of the past, the better to comprehend the contemporary political crisis. Amplified and modified by a wide range of other theoretical practices (postcolonial, feminist, Foucaultian, antiracist, queer), critical theory today is an expansive field of inquiry well suited to plumb the historically specific complex of political, economic, social, and psychic powers and effects generative of our frightening predicament. That said, critical theory has its own share of theoretical-methodological conundrums: Does a theoretical diagnosis of the origins of political crises require a foundational account of socially embedded rationality? If so, how would such an account look? Can a critical theory of society, which does not exempt itself from the range of social practices it takes as its proper subject matter, have an objective or only a perspectival ground? What, if anything, entitles the critical theorist to identify general features of contemporary social and economic life as pathological, repressive, or unjust? What sources of normativity can be invoked to support such a diagnosis? Is the rise of violently antidemocratic desires and political expressions best interpreted as an "unleashing" of psychic features that already existed or as a novel historical formation? The present volume offers three distinctive critical-theoretical perspectives on the current political situation. Each works from and within critical theory in its own way, and responds differently to these questions. The contributors treat critical theory not as a unified method or stable doctrine but as a situated practice of critique and analysis, drawing on the strength of the old, yet open to the new and the unthought. Above all, they regard critical theory as animated by an emancipatory purpose, manifested in ever changing forms as it encounters new problems in different regions of the world.

NEOLIBERALISM'S FRANKENSTEIN

AUTHORITARIAN FREEDOM IN
TWENTY-FIRST CENTURY "DEMOCRACIES"

Wendy Brown

"A new political science is needed for a world altogether new,"
Tocqueville famously wrote in 1835.[1] Tocqueville was not denying either the historicity of the new order or the relevance of
past thinkers to grasping it; his own work strongly featured both.
Rather, his point was that extant modes and categories of political
understanding could not capture the predicates, characteristics,
and dynamics comprising the most important political emergence of his time: democracy.

We face something similar today in the disintegration, or
at least transmogrification, of liberal democracy by forces for
which we do not yet have adequate names. I am not speaking
only of the eruption of extreme right movements and parties in
mainstream political life. How are we to theorize, or even characterize, the transformations of popular sovereignty forged by
novel fusions of social, political, technological, and economic
powers? To capture the dilutions of state sovereignty and the
disorienting interregnum between nation-states and whatever
their successors might be? To fathom the resurgence of religious forces in politics and the challenges to the identification
of liberal democracy with secularism? What is the bearing on
democratic commitments of the intensification of organized

nonstate transnational political violence? What of the extra-
ordinary new powers of digital communication—their effects
on political subjectivities, identities, allegiances, and alliances?
What kinds of subjects, societies, states, and political discourses
have emanated from four decades of neoliberal governmental-
ity and three decades of financialization? What is the effect on
democratic imaginaries of an unprecedentedly integrated and
complex global order, on the one hand, and the specter of planetary finitude, on the other?

The necessity of new theoretical vocabularies and registers to
apprehend these novel powers, constellations, and specters does
not consign the critical theory archive to the dustbin. It is in any
event impossible to invent, *de novo*, a critical theory of the Now,
and a foolish ambition to develop a *comprehensive* theoretical
account of our times. Nor can we simply lift ourselves by our
metaphysical bootstraps out of our learned ways of interpreting
the world, or substitute neologisms for the difficult work of theoretical insight. As we draw our extant critical theories toward
explaining the present, illumination may rest, paradoxically, in
drawing up short before what they cannot explain; in dwelling,
however uncomfortably, in that disorienting, even stupefying
place; in essaying experimental combinations and juxtapositions
of theorists and disciplines long been held apart by vigilantly po-
liced orthodoxies. A "new critical theory for a world itself quite
new" will require contributions from history, religion, anthro-
pology, political economy, social theory, and psychoanalysis as
well as politics and philosophy—each of which will in turn be
augmented by this breaking down of boundaries.

Opening to the novelties of our political age also brings into
focus the occlusions, and not just the supersession, of our own
previous work in critical theory. What powers did we fail to track
and thematize that have now exploded as enraged white masculinist nationalism in the context of global movements of capital
and peoples? Or have taken shape as plutocratic-populist alliances braided together by moralization and marketization? As
nihilistic mobilizations of "traditional" morality? As an antipoli-

tics releasing a ferocious will to power in politics? As disinhibited aggression in political and social life? Developing a new critical theory is daunting. Yet the inordinate privilege of being scholars of this world demands that we try, however haltingly and despite all risk of failure. The work will be inevitably haphazard and partial, always tethered by specific problems or questions and inflected by specific intellectual dispositions, knowledges, and limitations. In these ways, developing new critical theory for our new age is an inherently common project, albeit not necessarily a collective one.

The following is one very preliminary effort to theorize the emergence of "authoritarian freedom" today.

*
* *

I want to give France its freedom back. I want to take it out of jail. MARINE LE PEN, APRIL 2017

I joined UKIP because I believe it is the only party that truly values freedom and aspiration. UKIP is about more than independence from the EU. It is about independence from an Orwellian interventionist nanny state; it is about independence for the individual. It is the only party that believes in personal responsibility and equality of opportunity not of outcome. It is the only party that places trust in people not politicians and the bureaucratic class. ALEXANDRA SWANN, MARCH 2012[2]

I introduced my twenty-three-year-old law student daughter... to Milo [Yiannopoulos]'s videos, and she says he makes her feel relieved. And natural. And for me, he is like a loose flowery shirt in an all-plaid environment. NAME WITHHELD, PRIVATE CORRESPONDENCE WITH AUTHOR

A predominantly white, uneducated, evangelical Christian population, animated by discontent, rage, woundedness, or all three, brought Donald Trump to power.[3] Yes, he also drew support from some educated whites, racial minorities, the ultrarich, the ultra-Zionist, and the alt-right. But his electoral base was and remains white American voters without a college degree, many of whom forthrightly acknowledged that he was unqualified to be president.[4] He mobilized not simply class resentment but white rancor, especially white male rancor, provoked by lost pride of place (social, economic, cultural, and political) in the context of four decades of neoliberalism and globalization.

In fact, neoliberalism, and post-Fordism before it, have been far more devastating to the black American working class. In 1970 more than two-thirds of urban black workers had blue-collar jobs; by 1987 that had dropped to 28 percent.[5] In addition to rising un- and underemployment, poor and working-class black neighborhoods were hard hit by neoliberal defunding of public schools, services, and welfare benefits and by draconian sentencing mandates for nonviolent crimes. Together, these resulted in an exploding drug and gang economy, a catastrophic black incarceration rate, and a growing chasm between a small black middle class and the rest of African America.[6] But this devastation is the stuff of broken promises, not backward-looking rancor about lost supremacy or entitlement, not crushed political and social imagos of the self, the race, and the nation.

Clearly, white backlash against socioeconomic dethronement by neoliberal economic policy and what Marine Le Pen termed "savage globalization" is rampant across the Euro-Atlantic zone, where white working- and middle-class inhabitants, facing declining access to decent incomes, housing, schools, pensions, and futures, have risen up in political rebellion against both imagined dark usurpers and the cosmopolitans and elites they hold responsible for throwing open the doors of their nations and throwing them away. This much we know. But what is the political form of this anger and its mobilization? The old terms bandied about to describe it—populism, authoritarianism, fascism—fail to capture the strange brew of bellicosity, disinhibition, and an antidemocratic blend of license and support for statism in current political and social formations. Nor do they identify the specific elements of neoliberal reason—a radically extended reach of the private, mistrust of the political, and disavowal of the social, which together normalize inequality and disembowel democracy—that shape and legitimize these angry white right political passions. And they do not capture the deep nihilism that makes values into playthings, truth inconsequential, and the future a matter of indifference or, worse, an unconscious object of destruction.

In what follows, I explore this conjuncture from just one angle: what generates the antipolitical yet libertarian *and* authoritarian dimensions of popular right-wing reaction today? What novel iterations and expressions of freedom have been wrought from the conjuncture of neoliberal reason, aggrieved white male power, nationalism, and unavowed nihilism? How has freedom become the calling card and the energizing force of a formation so manifestly unemancipatory, routinely characterized as heralding "illiberal democracy" in its attacks on equal rights, civil liberties, constitutionalism, and basic norms of tolerance and inclusion, and in its affirmations of white nationalism, strong statism, and authoritarian leadership? How and why have freedom and illiberalism, freedom and authoritarianism, freedom and legitimized social exclusion and social violence, become fused in our time? How has this fusion developed its appeal and modest legitimacy in formerly liberal democratic nations? This essay does not provide the genealogy that would answer these questions comprehensively, but offers a first foray. It follows several historical tributaries and builds on the unlikely theoretical trio of Friedrich Hayek, Friedrich Nietzsche, and Herbert Marcuse: Hayek for an account of the political rationality of our time, Nietzsche and Marcuse for accounts of the rancorous, disinhibited, antisocial, and nihilistic aggression exploding within it.

THE LOGICS AND EFFECTS OF NEOLIBERAL REASON

Neoliberalism is commonly understood as a set of economic policies promoting unrestricted actions, flows, and accumulations of capital by means of low tariffs and taxes, deregulation of industries, privatization of formerly public goods and services, stripped-out welfare states, and the breakup of organized labor. Foucault and others have also taught us to grasp neoliberalism as a governing rationality generating distinctive kinds of subjects, forms of conduct, and orders of social meaning and value.[7] Different from ideology—a distortion or mystification of reality—neoliberal rationality is productive, world-making: it economizes every sphere and human endeavor, and it replaces a model of society based on the justice-producing social contract with a conception of society organized as markets and of states oriented by market requirements. As neoliberal rationality becomes our ubiquitous common sense, its principles not only govern through the state but suffuse workplaces, schools, hospitals, gyms, air travel, policing, and all manner of human desire and decisions. Higher education, for example, is reconfigured by neoliberal rationality as an investment by human capital in the enhancement of its own future value, a transformation that makes literally unintelligible the idea and practice of education as a democratic public good. Everything in universities is affected by this—tuition levels and budget priorities, of course, but also curricula, teaching and research practices, hiring and admissions criteria, and administrative concerns and conduct. The coordinates of ostensibly liberal democratic nations are similarly reformatted. For example, soon after his 2017 election, French prime minister Emmanuel Macron declared his determination to make France a nation that "thinks and moves like a startup."[8] Across the ocean, Jared Kushner, leader of the White House Office of American Innovation, tasked with "fixing government with business ideas," proclaimed, "The government should be run like a great American company. Our hope is that we can achieve successes and efficiencies for our customers, who are the citizens."[9]

What is the specific formulation of freedom carried by neoliberal reason? This varies across different thinkers and instantiations of neoliberalism, but some generalizations can be made. Most obviously, as freedom is submitted to market meanings, it is stripped of the political valences that attach it to popular sovereignty and thus to democracy. Instead, freedom is equated wholly with the pursuit of private ends, is appropriately unregulated, and is largely exercised to enhance the value, competitive positioning, or market share of a person or firm. Its sole political significance is negative: it flourishes where politics, and especially government, are absent. As neoliberal reason reconfigures freedom's meaning, subjects, and objects in this way, it denigrates the left as opposed to freedom *tout court*, not just in markets. A brief turn to the founding neoliberals will allow us to grasp this move more precisely.

Neoliberal thought was born in the shadow of European fascism and Soviet totalitarianism. However significant their epistemological and ontological differences, the Ordoliberal, Freiburg, and Chicago School thinkers who founded the Mont Pelerin Society shared the conviction that these dark formations were on a continuum with the pervasive social planning and state-managed political economies of their time. Keynesian welfare states, social democracy, and public ownership all lie on the "road to serfdom." They represent the related dangers of, on the one hand, elevating the notion of the social and conceiving nations in terms of society rather than individuals and, on the other, interfering with the spontaneous order of interdependence and need provision generated by giving individual liberty the widest possible berth.[10]

Why the attack on society and *the social*? For neoliberals, as Margaret Thatcher famously intoned, society does not exist. Thatcher's intellectual lodestar, Friedrich Hayek, decried "the social" as a term at once mythical, incoherent, and dangerous, falsely anthropomorphizing and drawing on animism too.[11] What makes belief in the realm of the social so nefarious for Hayek is that it inevitably leads to attempts to make justice and order by design. This in turn undermines the dynamic order delivered by the combination of markets and morals, neither of which emanate from reason or intention; rather, both spontaneously evolve.[12] Moreover, since justice pertains to conduct comporting with universal rules, it is a misnomer when applied to the condition or state of a people, as in the term "social justice." Social justice, then, is misguided, assaults freedom in spirit and in fact, and assaults traditional morality as it inevitably attempts to replace it with one group's idea of the Good.

Apart from its role in implementing misguided social policy, why do neoliberals also oppose *the political*? For Milton Friedman, the twin threat of political life to freedom rests in its inherent concentration of power, which markets disperse, and its fundamental reliance on coercion, whether by rule or dictate, whereas markets feature choice.[13] While he acknowledges that some measure of political power is indispensable for stable, secure societies and even for the existence and health of markets (property and contract law, monetary policy, and so forth), every political act, rule, or mandate is, for Friedman, a subtraction from individual freedom. Even direct democracy, whenever it falls short of unanimity, compromises freedom, as it imposes the will of the majority on the minority. Markets, by contrast, always allow individual preferences to prevail—the equivalent of always getting what one votes for rather than having to submit to majorities. Friedman writes:

> The political principle that underlies the market mechanism is unanimity. In an ideal free market resting on private property, no individual can coerce any other, all cooperation is voluntary, all parties to such cooperation benefit or they need not participate. There are no values, no "social" responsibilities in any sense other than the shared values and responsibilities of individuals. Society is a collection of individuals and of the various groups they voluntarily form. The political principle that underlies the political mechanism is conformity. The individual must serve a more general social interest—whether that be determined by a church or a dictator or a majority. The individual may have a vote and say in what is to be done, but if he is overruled, he must conform.[14]

Hayek, too, regarded political life as compromising individual liberty and the spontaneous order and progress it generates when disciplined (hence "responsibilized") by competition. This is more than a brief for limited government. Rather, for Hayek, politics as such, and democracy in particular, limit freedom as they concentrate power, constrain individual action, disrupt spontaneous order, and distort the natural incentives, distributions, and hence health of markets. In *Law, Legislation and Liberty*, he commences with this epigram from Walter Lippmann: "In a free society the state does not administer the affairs of men. It administers justice among men who conduct their own affairs."[15]

Yet even this way of putting the matter, insofar as it focuses on the state and economy, understates the texture and the venue of neoliberal freedom, in which deregulation and privatization become broad moral-philosophical principles extending well beyond the economy. As these principles take hold, constraints on freedom in the name of civility, equality, inclusion, or public goods, and above all in the name of what Hayek terms "the dangerous superstition" of social justice, are on a continuum with fascism and totalitarianism.[16] To understand this, we need to consider Hayek's stipulation of freedom more closely.

For Hayek, liberty prevails where there is no intentional human coercion; it is restricted only by enforced rules, dictates, or threats. Freedom, or liberty (he uses the terms interchangeably), is nothing more than "independence of the arbitrary will of another"; it "refers solely to a relation of men to other men, and the only infringement on it is coercion by men."[17] Hayek explicitly rejects every other meaning of freedom and is especially hostile to meanings that flirt with capacity or power to act—"freedom to"—or that equate freedom with popular sovereignty.[18] He considers these not merely wrong but dangerous insofar as they lead to an enlarged sense of entitlement and thus to state control in the form of resource distribution and social planning. Freedom conceived as agency, capacity, or sovereignty yields interventions that both limit true freedom and destroy the spontaneous order it generates. Put sharply, freedom pursued or practiced apart from its liberal market sense (this would include all left emancipation projects) inevitably inverts into freedom's opposite.

Why, according to Hayek, does a spontaneous order of interdependence and civilizational development emerge only in the absence of political intervention? Why this hostility toward experts, planners, and even complex legal orders? The answer rests with Hayek's theory of inherent social ignorance, his insistence that there is and can be no master knowledge of society, on the part either of individuals or of groups: "The case for individual freedom rests chiefly on the recognition of the inevitable ignorance of all of us concerning a great many of the factors on which the achievement of our ends and welfare depends.... [I]f there were omniscient men ... there would be little case for liberty."[19] For Hayek, the knowledge on which civilizations have been built is too widely disseminated and too deeply sedimented for it ever to be assembled and processed by anyone or any group, anywhere. Thus, a state indulging in social policy or planning will simultaneously make errors, curtail liberty, stymie the innovation and order that markets generate, and reduce discipline and hence responsibility. State planning or control is thus inherently oppressive, error-ridden, and socially devitalizing.[20] Liberty, by contrast, generates a kind of secular intelligent design *when* it is disciplined by the competition that responsibilizes liberty's use.

The root principle may be familiar from Adam Smith, but Hayek has significantly modified it and expanded its purview. As Foucault notes, the modification replaces exchange with competition as the engine of spontaneous order and development, and thus requires that competition be installed in every domain and instilled in every subject.[21] The expansion posits market liberty as a comprehensive ontological and normative principle: *all* society is like a market and best organized as a market, and all liberty (personal, political, social, civic) has a market form. This expansion is what builds an economic theory into a cosmological one: the same kind of freedom ought to prevail everywhere and is capable of producing the same positive effects everywhere. Liberty generates responsibility, responsibility generates discipline, and discipline generates social innovations, efficiencies, and order. The normative dimension of Hayek's theory animates the neoliberal constructivist project to make its principles ubiquitously governing ones.[22] But how does this normative project take hold? That is, how is freedom expanded to all domains of existence, and conversely, how are the reach and power of politics confined and reduced? The familiar answer is that this happens by privatizing public goods and responsibilizing subjects—the explicit mission of Thatcherism and Reaganism in the 1980s and 1990s, and of all neoliberal governance since.[23] Important as it is, however, economic privatization works at only one end of the problem that neoliberals aimed to solve, as it eliminates restrictions on freedom by eliminating government ownership and responsibilizing subjects and families through the dismantling of public provisions. More crucial for our purposes is Hayek's concern with *expanding* the reach and claim of what he calls "the personal, protected sphere" to curtail the reach of the political and dismantle claims of the social.[24] Here, fostering individual self-care is not the driving aim. Rather, this project of freedom involves designating more and more activity as private, hence appropriately unregulated *and* appropriately shielded from democratic norms. In Hayek's words, "the recognition of property" is "the first step in delimiting the private sphere protecting us against coercion," but "we must not think of this sphere as consisting exclusively, or even chiefly, of material things."[25] Rather, this sphere gives us "protection against interference with our actions." It walls out coercion, especially by that major coercive power, the state, but also by broadly diffused democratic norms such as equality, inclusion, access, and even civility. This is more than a project of privatizing public things; both the zone and objects of the private are expanded to contest the domain and power of liberty's enemies: political power and belief in the social.

In the United States, as neoliberal rationality has widened

and deepened its hold, this abstract principle of securing personal freedom against the presumed coerciveness of political life (including but not limited to state coercion) has unfolded concretely in both legislation and popular discourse. It is widely mobilized by the right to challenge norms of equality, tolerance, and inclusion in the name of freedom and choice. It has been deployed by the Supreme Court majority to enhance the power of corporations to monopolize and manipulate ever larger parts of political life while also granting them ever greater protection from political regulation and mandates, thereby converting neoliberal plutonomy into a novel, depoliticized form of plutocracy. It has taken shape in American jurisprudence as individual civil rights (for example, to unrestricted speech or religious conscience) are extended to corporations and as justice is privatized through the replacement of public, appealable court procedures with confidential, rigged-for-the-powerful binding arbitration.[26]

These practices of privatization do more than challenge principles and practices of equality and antidiscrimination. Expanding the "personal, protected sphere" is also a means of ushering *family* values, ordinances, and claims into public spaces heretofore organized by democratic law and norms. The social and the public are thus not only *economized* but *familialized* by neoliberalism: together these shifts challenge the principles of equality, secularism, pluralism, and inclusion at the heart of modern democratic society, allowing them to be replaced by what Hayek termed the "traditional moral values" of the "personal, protected sphere."[27] Consider, in this regard, the campaign, now three decades old, to replace public funding of education with individual vouchers that permit families to choose schools for their children that comport with their moral values and to escape schools that do not. Or consider court rulings permitting businesses to escape federal equality mandates on the basis of religious "belief," and so to withhold employee health insurance coverage for forms of contraception deemed abortifacients or refuse custom from LGBT people seeking to marry. Or consider the increasingly open identification of Western nations with Christianity, in centrist as well as conservative political discourse, and the compromise of a secular public sphere that this identification entails. In short, expanding the "personal, protected sphere" and curtailing the reach of democracy in the name of freedom develops a new ethos of the nation, one that replaces a public, pluralistic, secular democratic national imaginary with a private, homogenous, familial one.[28] The former features commitments to modest openness, the rule of law, and cultural and religious pluralism. The latter, especially in its traditional form, is exclusionary, walled, homogenous, unified, and hierarchical.

Neoliberal *economic* privatization is deeply subversive of democracy; it generates inequality, exclusion, private ownership of the commons, plutocracy, and a profoundly dimmed democratic imaginary.[29] The second order of privatization we have been considering, however, subverts democracy with antidemocratic moral or "family" values rather than antidemocratic capital values.[30] It wages familial rather than market warfare on democratic principles and institutions. It positions exclusion, patriarchalism, tradition, nepotism, and Christianity as legitimate challenges to inclusion, autonomy, equal rights, limits on conflicts of interest, secularism, and the very principle of equality.[31] Moreover, while both kinds of privatization are animated by a concern with freedom, the second is especially important in generating the political formation of an authoritarian freedom today. As the "personal, protected sphere" is empowered against the social and expands to envelop the nation itself, securing and protecting it requires increasingly robust statism in the form of law, policing, and defense.

We must avoid being blinded by the language of rights here. Rights attached to individuals are the flying wedge with which democratic commitments to equality, civility, and inclusion— "social justice"—are challenged by neoliberal reason instantiated as jurisprudence and public policy or wielded by alt-right activists under the banner of "free speech." The forces behind them, however, which stage incursions into public space and push back against the political and the democratic, are the values and claims of the market, on the one hand, and hetero-patriarchal Christian familialism, on the other. In each case, rights are strategically redeployed from their intended attachment to individuals to something else—corporations, property, capital, families, churches, whiteness. Economic and familial privatization of the public, combined with the neoliberal denigration of the social, together build the right-wing attack on "social justice" as tyrannical or fascist. Redress of historical injustices, even basic civil rights for racial and sexual minorities, women, and other subordinate groups, are rendered by neoliberalism as contrived and illegitimate dictates that draw on the "mirage of the social" and constitute both attacks on personal freedom and interference in the spontaneous order of markets and morals.[32] The charge is not just that these projects serve egalitarian rather than libertarian ends, a cardinal sin in any neoliberal playbook. It is not just that they impose a political vision of "the good society"—social engineering or social planning—where there should only be liberty, competition, and privatism. It is not just that they are political interventions—regulatory or redistributive—thwarting the proper organization of achievement and reward by markets. It is not just that they suppress the creative energies of free individuals and the spontaneous order those energies yield. And it is not just that they contravene traditional morality and limit the entitlement of families and churches to influence, if not control, civic life and discourse in neighborhoods, towns, and nations. Rather, these wrongs are together sculpted into the figure of a political Antichrist within a Hayekian formulation of freedom that valorizes and expands the private to retrench the reach of the political and challenge the very existence of the social.[33] Extending the purview of the private and applying the disintegrative force of deregulation to everything everywhere enables a novel practice of freedom to actualize the claim that "there is no such thing as society" as it assaults the values and the practices that sustain social bonds, social inclusion, social cooperation, social provision, and, of course, social equality.

At this point, it is easy to see how sometimes viciously sexist, transphobic, xenophobic, and racist speech and conduct have erupted as expressions of freedom, challenging the dictates of "political correctness." When the "personal, protected sphere" is extended, when opposition to restriction and regulation becomes a foundational and universal principle, when the social is demeaned and the political demonized, individual animus and the historical powers of white male dominance are both unleashed and legitimated. No one owes anything to anyone or has the right to restrict anyone in any way; equality, as Hayek bluntly declared, is but the language of envy.[34] Meanwhile, left opposition to supremacist sentiment is cast as tyrannical policing rooted in the totalitarian mythos of the social and drawing on the coercive powers of the political. The effect is to profoundly reframe, and not just reignite, the culture wars, once imagined to have peaked at the end of the twentieth century.[35]

I want to be very clear here. I am not claiming that Hayek or other neoliberals imagined or advocated for the disinhibited attacks on immigrants, Muslims, blacks, Jews, queers, and women enacted by an emboldened and growing radical right today. The point is, rather, that these developments are in part effects of neoliberal reason—its expansion of the domain and claim of the private for persons and corporations alike, and its rejection of political and social (as opposed to market) justice. If, as Andrew Lister argues, Hayek's "critique of social or distributive justice has a very narrow target"—economic intervention in market outcomes by the state—its scope widened as it became part of the political rationality of our time. Moreover, the displacement of the social and the attack on the political, along with the broad discrediting of democratic norms, fueled and legitimated energies emanating from an entirely different set of concrete neoliberal effects—namely the declining sovereignty and security of men, whites, Christianity, and nation-states. These energies of aggrieved power are expressed variously (in rancorous rage and acting out but also in quiet voting for far-right candidates) and target a range of objects (politicians and liberal elites, in addition to those named above). But they would not have a legitimate political form in a liberal or social democratic order, which is why they remained on the political fringe until recent years. Neoliberal reason's assault on egalitarianism, social provision, social justice, politics, and democracy, along with its extension of the "personal, protected sphere," has given them that legitimate form. We are thus dealing with what Stuart Hall would call a "conjuncture" or what Foucault would term a "contingent genealogical formation."

We will scrutinize these novel energies carefully in a moment. First, however, we are now positioned to comprehend one of the more perplexing features of the current landscape, namely how the right can be the party of both freedom *and* nationalism, freedom *and* protectionism, maximized personal liberty *and* traditional social values. When the twin dimensions of privatization we have been considering discursively capture the nation itself, it ceases to be figured primarily as a democracy but instead is figured, on the one hand, as a competitive business needing to make good deals and attract investors and, on the other, as an inadequately secured home, besieged by ill-willed or nonbelonging outsiders. Contemporary right-wing nationalism oscillates between the two. Consider Trump's continual braying about America's recent history of bad international deals, on everything from trade to NATO to climate accords, alongside his depiction of the United States as undermined by its unsecured borders and his campaign promise to build a wall featuring a "great big, beautiful door" through which legal entrants from the south may visit or join "our family."[36] Or consider Marine Le Pen's "France for the French" campaign, which combined economic and familial languages to depict the nation: "We are the owners of our country," she declared at a rally in eastern France, and "we must have the keys to open the house of France, to open it halfway, [or] to close the door." "It is our house," the crowd chanted back.[37] As one supporter explained, "She's not against immigrants, only securing justice.... It's like when the refrigerator is full we give to our neighbors, but when the refrigerator is empty we give to our children. The refrigerator of France is empty."[38] Justice is reformatted as the titrated hospitality of a private household.

When the nation itself is economized and familialized in this way, democratic principles of universality, equality, and openness are jettisoned, and the nation becomes legitimately illiberal toward those designated as aversive insiders or invading outsiders. Statism, policing, and authoritarian power also ramify since walling, policing, and securitization of every kind are authorized by the need to secure this vast expanse of personal, deregulated freedom. Security is not what guarantees or limits freedom; rather, walls, gates, security systems, and No Trespassing signs become freedom's signifiers as they demarcate the private from the public, the protected from the open, the familiar from the strange, the owned from the common. Democratic procedure and legitimacy are displaced by the values of the family and the market: not negotiation, deliberation, or even the rule of law but *diktat* is the basis of household authority, and force is how it legitimately defends itself against intruders. Securing a vast expanse of the private, and of deregulated freedom, thus inaugurates new spaces and valorizations of policing, authority, and securitization, the need for which is intensified by the disinhibited social energies we shall consider shortly.[39] *Et voilà*—twenty-first-century authoritarianism in freedom's name!

THE ENERGIES OF RIGHT-WING FREEDOM
AND NATIONALISM

To this point, we have been considering a *logic* of governing reason, but not the affective energies giving shape and content to contemporary rightist political formations and expressions. Neoliberal reason by itself, including its rollout in law and policy and its interpellation of subjects, does not generate nationalist movements hell-bent on whitening nations, walling out immigrants and refugees, or vilifying feminists, queers, liberals, leftists, intellectuals, and even mainstream journalists. Nor does it incite rancorous rage and other antisocial passions, or pop the lid on the worst of "human nature," masculinity, or whiteness.[40] Here what is important are not the broad shifts occasioned by neoliberal reason, as outlined above, but the effects of neoliberal economic policy in specific historical-social contexts, especially those that trammel white middle- and working-class existence in rural and suburban regions of Euro-Atlantic nations. Let us briefly reprise the familiar:

Both right and left political energies today are responses, in part, to the neoliberal dismantling of livable incomes, job security, retirement provisions, and publicly funded education, services, and other social goods. These effects are compounded by neoliberal trade, tax, and tariff policies that both undermine nation-state sovereignty and produce a global race to the bottom in wages and public revenues. Inchoately, until right-wing nationalist party platforms made it choate, many dethroned working- and middle-class whites in Europe and North America sensed a connection between the decline of nation-state sovereignty, their own declining economic well-being, and declining white male supremacy. And they are right: undone by offshored union factory jobs, disappearing affordable housing, and unprecedented global movements of labor and capital, the age of the secure white male provider *and* nation-state sovereignty in the Global North is finished. This condition cannot be reversed but can be politically instrumentalized. Here, the hyperbolized figure of the immigrant is especially potent, where the terrorist fuses with the job-stealer, criminal, and neighborhood malingerer, and where, conversely, false promises of restored economic potency mix with false promises of restored racial and gender supremacy. Porous boundaries of neighborhood and nation, eroded socioeconomic status, and new forms of insecurity are braided together in a racialized causal logic *and* economized redress. As the Brexit slogan had it, "We will control our country again." Or the French again: "It is our house."

Yet it is a mistake to see *white* working- and middle-class men as uniquely injured by neoliberal policy and uniquely neglected by neoliberal politicians. This common reproach of the Hillary Clinton campaign by mainstream liberal pundits—that it focused too much on identity politics and gave short shrift to the white working stiff—misses the extent to which the displacement suffered by whites, and especially white men, is mainly experienced not as economic decline but as lost entitlement to politically, socially, and economically reproduced supremacism. It fails to grasp, therefore, why right-wing and plutocratic politicians can get away with doing nothing substantive for their constituencies as long as they verbally anoint their wounds with anti-immigrant, antiblack, and antiglobalization rhetoric, and as long as they realign the figure and voice of the nation with the figure and voice of nativism. Again, whether targeting multiculturalists, political elites, liberal academics, refugees, feminists, or Black Lives Matter activists, right-wing rage against "political correctness" and "social justice" is fueled by the dethronement of whites, especially white men, across class.[41] By themselves, neither neoliberal expansions of the private nor neoliberal devastations of economic and political security generate the ferocious energies of racist nationalism and the freedom cry through which it is born: this third ingredient is necessary. Contemporary right-wing outbursts of misogyny, racism, Islamophobia, and anti-immigrant vigilantism were not simply "there" all along, the seamy underside of civilization suddenly released into the social-political libidosphere, licensed and mobilized by opportunistic politicians, and given an easy platform by social media. Rather, these outbursts carry the specific resentments and rage of aggrieved power.

The master philosopher of aggrieved power, of course, is Nietzsche. There is, to begin with, his account of how suffering, especially the suffering of humiliation, when routed through *ressentiment*, becomes moralizing condemnation of the object it holds responsible. In his formulation of what he called slave morality, Nietzsche focused mainly on the pious self-valorization of the meek and weak, and their denunciation of the strong and powerful. Yet he recognized that slave morality was also practiced by bombastic haters, anti-Semites and racists, diagnosing the swagger and slugging of such types as part of the order of "reactive feelings . . . grudges and rancor."[42] Mob-ism, bullying, bellicosity—Nietzsche castigated these grievous, resentful energies as opposites to the self-overcoming, proud, world-making energies of the powerful and creative that he affirmed.

Certainly *ressentiment* is a vital energy of right-wing populism: rancor, grudges, barely concealed victimization, and other affective qualities of *reaction* are the affective heartbeat of internet trolling, tweets, and speeches at right-wing rallies, and a striking feature of Trump's own demeanor. For philosopher Hans Sluga, however, Nietzsche's most important contribution to theorizing the current conjuncture is his treatment of nihilism.[43] Often mischaracterized as a nihilist because he reckoned with the contingent nature of values and truth, Nietzsche is more properly appreciated as a philosopher of the age of nihilism, which he knew to be unfolding in the centuries after science and reason topple God and shatter the foundations of every moral and ethical truth. As Sluga reminds us, for Nietzsche the age of nihilism does not mean the elimination of values but a world in which "the highest values devaluate themselves" as they become unmoored from their foundations.[44] Western Judeo-Christian values, including those that secure liberal democracy, lose their depth as they lose their fundaments; accordingly, they do not vanish but become fungible and trivial, easily traded, augmented, instrumentalized, superficialized. These effects further degrade the value of values, inevitably deepening the nihilism of cultures and their subjects.

There is ubiquitous evidence of this phenomenon today. It is quotidian in the instrumentalization of values for commercial and political gain—"branding"—and in the general lack of umbrage at this instrumentalization. It is manifest in a US Supreme Court majority that pretends to "originalism" while stretching the Constitution to sanction everything from torture to corporate personhood.[45] It is evident in a survey of American voters, conducted in October 2011 and repeated five years later: in 2011, during the Obama presidency, only 30 percent of white evangelical Protestants believed that an elected official who commits an immoral act in his or her personal life can still behave ethically in public and professional life; this figure rose to 72 percent in October 2016, when Trump was a candidate. Similarly, in 2011, 64 percent of white evangelicals considered it very important for a presidential candidate to have strong religious beliefs, a figure that dropped to 49 percent during the Trump campaign.[46] These changes were surely the effect less of deep ethical reflection than of shifting political tides. This is how nihilism goes—not the death of values but their becoming protean, becoming available for branding projects and covering purposes that manifestly do not comport with them.

Not only values but truth and reason lose their moorings in a nihilistic age.[47] Truth, still hoisted, ceases to require evidence or even reasoning; constant shouts of "fake news" are effective, and highly sectoralized populations are fed accounts of events aimed at their established convictions. Yet convictions themselves are increasingly detached from faith and are immune to argumentation; they barely conceal their emanation from resentment, impulse, or outrage. Exemplified by the British tabloids whipping up Brexit support, nihilism's most notorious expression in this regard is Trump's manifest indifference to truth, consistency, or affirmative (as opposed to grievance-based) political or moral convictions. That Trump's supporters and most right-wing media largely share this indifference underscores the nihilistic character of the age.

For Sluga, Trumpism embodies another feature of nihilism

as Nietzsche depicts it, one crucial to freedom's antisocial qualities today. This is the desublimation of the will to power.[48] Both
Freud and Nietzsche understand values and the world built to
comport with them as sublimations of what Freud called the instincts or drives and Nietzsche termed the will to power. Both
understood the untamed human animal to be freer, in some ways
happier, in the absence of such sublimation, but also at risk of
self- and other-destruction. Above all, both understood civilization itself to be the product of sublimation. With nihilism's
devaluation of values, there is, Sluga argues, "a falling back and
collapse of the will to power into its own elementary form. . . .
[E]ven religion and the appeal to religious values become cyni-
cal instruments for the unrestrained use of power."[49] More is at
stake in this collapse than the exercise of power unbridled by
ethics or humility. Rather, Sluga writes, "what goes by the way
in this unrestrained will to power is any concern for others . . . in
particular the compact between generations on which our entire
social order has rested so far."[50] Sluga thus helps us understand
an aspect of right-wing freedom unyoked from conscience, not
just because it is contoured by neoliberal selfishness and critiques
of the social, but because of nihilism's own radical depression of
conscience.[51] Combined with the disparagement and depletion of
the social, freedom becomes doing or saying what one likes without regard for its effects, freedom to be genuinely without care
for the predicaments, vulnerabilities, or fates of other humans,
other species, or the planet. It is freedom, as Nietzsche puts it, to
"wreak one's will" for the sheer pleasure of it. And when this will
is wounded and rancorous from social castration or humiliation,
it is, as Elizabeth Anker formulates it, "ugly freedom."[52] At the
same time, however, Nietzsche would remind us of this freedom's
"festive quality"—it delights in the pleasures of provocation and
piling on, of humiliating others or making them suffer ("as one
has suffered"), of dancing at the bonfires of what one is burning
down.[53] This glee was manifest in some Brexiters, is ubiquitous
in right-wing blogs and trolling, and can be spied in the pleasure
of making liberals squirm when they are defeated by rulings and

policies that unleash the raw power of capital, fossil fuels, the right to bear arms, and more.

However, festivals of freedom celebrating the burning down of civilization or the future of the planet are not the worst of the matter. Rather, in this consequential turn, freedom abandons all of the affinity with political self-determination found in Rousseau, Tocqueville, or Marx; it departs the categorical imperative of Kant; it is untethered from Mill's cultivation of individuality and advancement of civilization; it even leaves behind Bentham's binding of liberty to the calculation of maximized utility. Instead, the nihilistic disintegration of ethical values combined with neoliberalism's assault on the social and the unleashing of the right and the power of the personal generates a freedom that is furious, passionate, and destructive—symptomizing ethical destitution even as it sometimes dresses in conservative righteousness. This freedom is paradoxically expressed as nihilism and as against nihilism, attacking and destroying while faulting its objects of derision for the ruin of traditional values and order. It is freedom unbridled and uncultured, freedom to put a stick in the eye of accepted norms, freedom from care of the morrow, joyous in its provocations and animated by aggrieved, vengeful reactions against those it holds responsible for its suffering or displacement. It is the freedom of "I will because I can, and I can because I am nothing, I believe in nothing and the world has become nothing."[54] This is the freedom remaindered by nihilism, in the making for centuries, and embodied in neoliberal reason itself, which posits no value apart from that generated by price and speculative markets.

REPRESSIVE DESUBLIMATION AND THE DEPRESSION OF CONSCIENCE

Not quite a century after Nietzsche wrote, Herbert Marcuse considered desublimation from a different angle, theorizing the nonliberatory release of instinctual energies in postwar capitalism. What Marcuse famously termed "repressive desublimation" occurs within an order of capitalist domination, exploitation, and "false needs" as technology reduces the demands of necessity and desire is everywhere incorporated into a commodity culture enjoyed by a growing middle class.[55] This order features plenty of pleasure, including that obtained by way of radically reduced strictures on sexuality (less grueling work requires less sublimation), but not emancipation. Instinctual energies, rather than being directly opposed by the mandates of society and economy, and thus requiring heavy repression and sublimation, are now coopted by and for capitalist production and marketing. As pleasure, and especially sexuality, are everywhere incorporated into capitalist culture, the pleasure principle and the reality principle slip their ancient antagonism.[56] Pleasure, instead of being an insurrectionary challenge to the drudgery and exploitation of labor, becomes capital's tool and generates submission.[57] Far from dangerous or oppositional, no longer sequestered in aesthetics or utopian fantasy, pleasure becomes part of the machinery. This much is familiar. Marcuse's next turn in developing the implications of repressive desublimation, however, bears most directly on our problem. According to Marcuse, nonliberatory desublimation facilitates "happy consciousness," Hegel's term for resolving the conflict between desire and social requirements by aligning one's consciousness with the regime. Marcuse draws on Freud and Marx to radicalize Hegel's formulation: in ordinary cultures of domination, he argues, "unhappy consciousness" is the effect of conscience—superegoic condemnation of "evil" urges in both self and society.[58] Conscience is thus at once an element in the superego's arsenal for internal restraint and a source of moral judgment about society. As repressive desublimation offers a reprieve from this strict censorship and gives rise to "happy consciousness" (a less divided self because a less conscientiously repressed one), conscience is the first casualty. Importantly, conscience relaxes not just in relation to the subject's own conduct but in relation to social wrongs and ills—*which are no longer registered as such*. In other words, less repression in this context leads to a less demanding superego, which means less conscience, which, in an individualistic, unemancipated society, means less ethical-political concern across the board. In Marcuse's words, "Loss of conscience due to the satisfactory liberties granted by an unfree society makes for a *happy consciousness* which facilitates acceptance of the misdeeds of this society. [This loss of conscience] is the token of declining autonomy and comprehension."[59]

That desublimation lessens the force of conscience makes intuitive sense, but why does Marcuse associate this with the subject's declining autonomy and intellectual comprehension? His complex point here differs from Freud's argument, in *Group Psychology and the Analysis of the Ego*, that conscience is reduced when the subject effectively transfers it to an idealized leader or authority. For Marcuse, autonomy declines when comprehension declines (this is the cognitivist, if not the rationalist, in him), and comprehension declines when it is not required for survival *and* when the unemancipated subject is steeped in capitalist commodity pleasures and stimuli. Put the other way around, instinctual repression takes work, including the work of the intellect.[60] Therefore, as late capitalist desublimation relaxes demands against the instincts but does not free the subject for self-direction, demands for intellection are substantially relaxed.[61] Free, stupid, manipulable, absorbed by if not addicted to trivial stimuli and gratifications, the subject of repressive desublimation in advanced capitalist society is not just libidinally unbound, released to enjoy more pleasure, but released from more general expectations of social conscience and social comprehension. This release is amplified by the neoliberal assault on the social and the depression of conscience fostered by nihilism.

Repressive desublimation, Marcuse argues, is "part and parcel of the society in which it happens but nowhere its negation."[62] It looks like freedom while shoring up the status quo and submitting to it. Its expressions, he says, may be bold or vulgar enough even to appear as maverick or dissident—it may be "wild and obscene, virile and tasty, quite immoral."[63] However, this daring and disinhibition (again, manifest in alt-right tweets, blogs, trolling, and performances) symptomize or iterate rather than counter the order's violence and prejudices, as well as its ordinary values.[64] In Marcuse's view, repressive desublimation twins "freedom and oppression," transgression and submission, in a distinctive way, as is apparent in the wild, raging, even outlaw expressions of patriotism and nationalism that frequently erupt from the extreme right today.[65]

Repressive desublimation unleashes new levels and perhaps even new forms of violence by opening the spigot of that other well of human instinct, Thanatos. Desublimation of Eros is compatible, Marcuse argues, "with the growth of unsublimated as well as sublimated forms of aggressiveness."[66] Why? Because repressive desublimation doesn't release Eros for freedom *tout court* but instead involves a compression or concentration of erotic energy at the site of sexuality—this is part of what makes it "controlled" or "repressive" desublimation. Desublimated Eros may, therefore, bestir, blend with, and even intensify aggression. Thus Marcuse explains growing accommodation or acquiescence to social and political violence—a "degree of normalization where... individuals are getting used to the risk of their own dissolution and disintegration."[67] His own reference was to the mid-twentieth-century Cold War buildup of nuclear weapons , but the point is easily adapted for climate change and other existential threats. Most importantly for our purposes, his insight is suggestive for understanding the quantity and intensity of aggression spilling from the right, especially the alt-right, amid its frenzied affirmation of individual freedom.

Finally, there is Marcuse's account of the role of the market in intensifying the nihilism theorized by Nietzsche. Writing well before the neoliberal revolution, Marcuse argues that the market has become both reality principle and moral truth: "The people are led to find in the productive apparatus [the market] the effective agent of thought and action to which their personal thought and action can and must be surrendered.... [I]n this transfer, the apparatus also assumes the role of a moral agent. Conscience is absolved by reification, by the general necessity of things. In this general necessity, guilt has no place."[68] Already depleted by desublimation's yielding of happy consciousness, the weak remains of conscience are taken over by market reason and market requirements. The real is both the rational and the moral. At once reality principle, imperative, and moral order, capitalism becomes necessity, authority, and truth rolled into one, suffusing every sphere and immune from criticism despite its manifest devastations, incoherencies, and instabilities. There is no alternative.

CONCLUSION

Let us gather these strands into a preliminary understanding of the formation of antidemocratic and antisocial authoritarian freedom taking shape today. We began with neoliberal reason's attack on the social and the political. Neoliberalism indicts the social as a fiction through which equality is pursued at the expense of the spontaneous order generated by markets and morals. It indicts the political as pretending to knowledge and making use of coercion where, in fact, ignorance prevails and freedom should reign. A depoliticized, antiregulatory state that provides support for extension of the personal sphere is forwarded as the antidote to these dangers. However, the effect of this antidote is to de-democratize political culture and to discredit norms and practices of inclusion, pluralism, tolerance, and equality. Advocacy of these norms and practices is cast by neoliberal reason as a wrongheaded effort that spurns freedom, replaces morals with political mandates, and engages the social engineering that builds totalitarianism. Hence the labeling of "social justice warriors" as "fascists" by the alt-right.

Moreover, as the expansion of markets and morals displaces discourses of society and democracy, the nation itself comes to be figured as owned rather than constituted by democratic citizenship. This ownership has a double face—that of a business aimed solely at making savvy deals and avoiding giveaways, and that of a home that must be secured in a dangerous world. Together these legitimate internal and external illiberalism, nativist nationalism, and even authoritarianism. Freedom becomes a weapon against the needful or historically excluded and paradoxically solicits the growth of statist power in the form of paternal protectionism, both economic and securitarian.

Much of this is the inadvertent rather than the intended progeny of the neoliberal intellectuals, who dreamed of nations comprising free individuals lightly restrained by the rule of law, guided by moral and market rules of conduct, and disciplined by competition. Just as Marxism's fatal flaw was its neglect of the enduring complexities of political power (dismissed as derivative or superstructural by Marx), the neoliberal dream has inverted into its own nightmare—authoritarian political culture supported by angry, myth-mongering masses. This is partly because neoliberals ignored the historically specific powers and energies in the realm whose very existence they denied, the social. It is partly due to their inadequate appreciation of the political, and especially state, powers that would take shape in the wake of dismantled democratic restraints on the state and the takeover of political life by corporate titans and finance. It is also partly due to the neoliberals' failure to understand how antidemocratic, antisocial, and destructive political passions could be nourished by neoliberalism's own principles, and would not be held back by a moral fabric increasingly thinned by nihilism.

From Nietzsche we drew an appreciation of how this novel iteration of freedom is inflected by humiliation, rancor, and the complex effects of nihilism. Aggrieved by the socioeconomic displacements of neoliberalism and globalization, the reactive creature of a nihilistic age, with its desublimated will to power, is spurred to aggressions unfettered by concern for truth, for society, or for the future. Nihilistic energies intensify the spirit of social disintegration in neoliberalism's savaging of the social contract as these energies license the feelings, desires, and prejudices emanating from deracination and displacement of historic entitlements of race and gender. "Make America Great Again" and "France for the French" barely bother to code themselves as anything more than masculinist, white-supremacist last gasps or grasps. Value-slinging in a nihilistic age, however, is not held to rigorous theological or philosophical standards.

Marcuse's account of repressive desublimation in "advanced capitalism" adds another aspect to the formation. Unlike the conservative, authority-oriented subject guided by conscience and closely identified with the rectitude of church and state, the reactionary subject of repressive desublimation is largely indifferent to ethics or justice. Malleable and manipulable, depleted of autonomy, moral self-restraint, and social comprehension, this subject is pleasure-mongering, aggressive, and perversely attached to the destructiveness and domination of its milieu. Radically disinhibited but without intellection or moral compass in regard to itself or to others, this subject's experience of thinned or ruptured, subjectively felt social ties and obligations is affirmed by neoliberal culture itself. Its disinhibition is contoured as aggression by that culture, by its wounds and their imagined source, and by the desublimations incited or invited by nihilism.

Behold the aggrieved, reactive creature fashioned by neoliberal reason and its effects, who embraces freedom without the social contract, authority without democratic legitimacy, and vengeance without values or futurity! Far from the calculating, entrepreneurial, moral, and disciplined being imagined by Hayek and his intellectual kin, this one is angry, amoral, and impetuous, spurred by unavowed humiliation and thirst for revenge. The intensity of this energy is tremendous on its own, and easily exploited by plutocrats, right-wing politicians, and tabloid media moguls intent on whipping it up and keeping it stupid. It does not need to be addressed by policy that might produce its concrete betterment because it seeks mainly psychic anointment of its wounds. For this same reason it cannot be easily pacified—it is fueled mainly by rancor and nihilistic despair. It cannot be appealed to by reason, facts, or sustained argument because it does not want to know, and it is unmotivated by consistency or depth in its values or by belief in truth. Its conscience is weak, while its sense of victimization and persecution runs high. It cannot be wooed by a viable alternative future, where it sees no place for itself, no prospect for restoring its lost supremacy. The freedom it champions has gained credence as the needs, urges, and values of the private have become legitimate forms of public life and public expression. Having nothing to lose, its nihilism does not simply negate but is festive and even apocalyptic, willing to take Britain over a cliff, deny climate change, support manifestly undemocratic powers, or put an unstable know-nothing in the most powerful position on earth, because it has nothing else. It probably cannot be reached or transformed yet also has no endgame. But what to do with it? And might we also need to examine the ways these logics and energies organize aspects of left responses to contemporary predicaments?

NOTES

An earlier version of this essay appears in *Critical Times* 1, no. 1 (2018): 60–79, http://ctjournal.org/index.php/criticaltimes/article/view/12. For their help with research, I am grateful to William Callison and Brian Judge

1. Tocqueville, *Democracy in America*, trans. Mansfield and Winthrop, p. 7.
2. Alexandra Swann, "Leaving the Tories for Ukip Was about Freedom and Aspiration." *Guardian*, March 6, 2012, https://www.theguardian.com/commentisfree/2012/mar/06/leaving-tories-ukip-alexandra-swann.
3. Eighty-eight percent of Trump voters were white in a nation where whites comprise 62 percent of the population. He was sup-

ported by over half of white female voters, two-thirds of white male voters, and almost two-thirds of white voters over the age of fifty. Alec Tyson and Shiva Maniam, "Behind Trump's Victory: Divisions by Race, Gender, Education." *Fact Tank*, November 9, 2016, http://www.pewresearch.org/fact-tank/2016/11/09/behind-trumps -victory-divisions-by-race-gender-education/; http://www.cnn .com/election/results/exit-polls.

4. Trump won the support of two-thirds of white voters who had no college degree. Nate Silver, "Education, Not Income, Predicted Who Would Vote for Trump," *FiveThirtyEight*, November 22, 2016, http://fivethirtyeight.com/features/education-not-income -predicted-who-would-vote-for-trump/. Somewhere between a fifth and a quarter of Trump voters interviewed in exit polls said that they did not think Trump was qualified for the presidency, suggesting that his anointing of their frustrations, anger, prejudice, or rank hatred was decisive. See Laura Roberts, "Why Did So Many White Women Vote for Donald Trump?" *Fortune*, November 17, 2016.

5. Adam Shatz, "Out of Sight, Out of Mind," *London Review of Books*, May 4, 2017, https://www.lrb.co.uk/v39/n09/adam-shatz /out-of-sight-out-of-mind.

6. Heather Gilligan, "It's the Black Working Class—Not White—That Was Hit Hardest by Industrial Collapse," *Timeline*, May 18, 2017, https://timeline.com/its-the-black-working-class-not -white-that-was-hit-hardest-by-industrial-collapse-1a6eea50f9f0.

7. Building on Michel Foucault's lectures in the *Birth of Biopolitics: Lectures at the Collège de France, 1978–1979*, ed. Michael Senellart, trans. Graham Burchell (New York: Picador, 2008), I have offered a précis of this rationality in Brown, *Undoing the Demos: Neoliberalism's Stealth Revolution* (New York: Zone, 2015).

8. See Angela Charlton, "Macron Launches 'French Tech Visa' Program to Woo Tech Industry, Build 'Startup Nation,'" *Business Insider*, June 16, 2017. http://www.businessinsider.com/macron -launches-french-tech-visa-program-to-woo-tech-industry-build -startup-nation-2017-6.

9. Ashley Parker and Phillip Rucker, "Trump Taps Kushner to Lead a SWAT Team to Fix Government with Business Ideas." *Washington Post*, March 26, 2017, https://www.washingtonpost .com/politics/trump-taps-kushner-to-lead-a-swat-team-to-fix -government-with-business-ideas/2017/03/26/9714a8b6-1254-11e7 -ada0-1489b735b3a3_story.html.

10. Certain Ordoliberals are exempt from this characterization. See Thomas Biebricher and Frieder Vogelmann, *The Birth of Auster- ity: German Ordoliberalism and Contemporary Neoliberalism* (Lan- ham, MD: Rowman & Littlefield, 2017).

11. F. A. Hayek, *The Fatal Conceit: The Errors of Socialism*, ed. W. W. Bartley III (Chicago: University of Chicago Press, 1988), 108, 112–13; Hayek, *Law, Legislation and Liberty: A New Statement of the Liberal Principles of Justice and Political Economy* (London: Routledge and Kegan Paul, 1982), 2:75–76.

12. Hayek, *Fatal Conceit*, 67, 116–17; Hayek, *Law, Legislation and Liberty*, 66–68.

13. Milton Friedman with Rose D. Friedman, *Capitalism and Freedom* (Chicago: University of Chicago Press, 2002), chap. 1.

14. Milton Friedman, "The Social Responsibility of Business Is to Increase Profits," *New York Times Magazine*, September 13, 1970, 12.

15. Walter Lippmann, *An Inquiry into the Principles of a Good Society* (Boston: Little, Brown, 1937), 267, quoted in Hayek, *Law, Legislation and Liberty*, v.

16. Hayek, *Law, Legislation and Liberty*, 66.

17. F. A. Hayek, *The Constitution of Liberty* (Chicago: University of Chicago Press, 1960), 59–60.

18. Hayek, *Constitution of Liberty*, 61–68.

19. Hayek, *Constitution of Liberty*, 80–81.

20. See Hayek, *Constitution of Liberty*, chap. 2, "The Creative Powers of a Free Civilization," esp. 75–90.

21. Foucault, *Birth of Biopolitics*, 118.

22. It is constructivist in the sense that neoliberals understand economization and marketization of new spheres not as occurring

naturally but as a project involving law, incentivization, and new forms of governance.

23. A sterling example is President Bill Clinton's Personal Responsibility and Work Opportunity Reconciliation Act (PRWORA, 1996), which aimed "to replace public responsibility for the welfare of poor women with a state-enforced system of private family responsibility." For a superb discussion, see Melinda Cooper, *Family Values: Between Neoliberalism and the New Social Conservatism* (New York: Zone, 2016), 63. Cooper reminds us that the act made biological paternity, no matter how distant from any actual social or legal relation to the mother or child, a lifelong financial responsibility for the "father" so as to relieve the state of this responsibility.

24. Hayek, *Constitution of Liberty*, 207.

25. Hayek, *Constitution of Liberty*, 207.

26. The project of empowering the private against democracy through the discourse of freedom is patently evident in First Amendment jurisprudence in the United States. In 2015, John C. Coates IV, a Harvard professor of business law, released a study demonstrating empirically what was obvious to any newspaper-reading citizen: "corporations have increasingly [and with growing speed] displaced individuals as direct beneficiaries of First Amendment rights." Coates. "Corporate Speech and the First Amendment: History, Data and Implications," http://papers.ssrn.com/sol3/papers.cfm?abstract_id=2566785, p. 1. Other legal scholars have offered convergent accounts with different political emphases. In a 2013 article in the *New Republic*, Tim Wu writes, "Once the patron saint of protesters and the disenfranchised, the First Amendment has become the darling of economic libertarians and corporate lawyers who have recognized its power to immunize private enterprise from legal restraint." Wu, quoted in Adam Liptak, "First Amendment, 'Patron Saint' of Protestors, Is Embraced by Corporations," *New York Times*, March 24, 2015, http://www.nytimes.com/2015/03/24/us/first-amendment-patron-saint-of-protesters-is-embraced-by-corporations.html. Burt Neuborne argues that the trend emerged in the 1970s and 1980s because "robust free-speech protec-

tion fit neatly into the right's skeptical, deregulatory approach to government generally, and . . . encouraged vigorous transmission by powerful speakers of the right's newly energized collection of ideas." Neuborne, *Madison's Music: On Reading the First Amendment* (New York: New Press, 2015).

The extension of free speech rights to corporations has empowered them to dominate the electoral process, as in the infamous 2010 *Citizens United* decision, and has been especially useful to heavily disparaged quarters of big business: the pharmaceutical, tobacco, coal, industrial meat, and airline industries have all made extensive use of free-speech challenges to advertising restrictions. It has also granted religious freedom to businesses large and small that wish to reject gay marriage or withhold employee insurance coverage for methods of birth control they believe to be un-Christian. The Trump administration has moved quickly to expand the right of businesses to evade antidiscrimination and equal protection provisions in the name of religious free expression, and to expand the rights of religious institutions to act politically while maintaining their nonprofit status. The rubric is freedom, the ruse is corporations rendered as persons, and the project is rolling back restrictions and mandates of all kinds.

27. "Social justice," Hayek wrote, generates "destruction of the indispensable environment in which the traditional moral values alone can flourish, namely personal freedom." *Law, Legislation and Liberty*, 67.

28. There is some irony in this as the sequel to the "nanny state" loathed by neoliberals.

29. This is the subject of *Undoing the Demos*.

30. Cooper, *Family Values*.

31. Sometimes, of course, these are combined: Clinton's previously mentioned "welfare reform," PRWORA, is an example.

32. Hayek, *Law, Legislation and Liberty*, 67.

33. Hayek deemed social justice a "semantic fraud," a "dangerous superstition," "that incubus which makes fine sentiments the instruments for the destruction of all values of a free civilization," and most tellingly as generating "the destruction of the indispens-

able environment in which the traditional moral values alone can flourish, namely personal freedom." See *Law, Legislation and Liberty*, 67–70.

34. Hayek, *Constitution of Liberty*, 155–56.

35. The left is not immune to this displacement of public by personal values and concerns, as is manifest in concerns with safe spaces and trigger warnings.

36. Kevin Johnson, "Trump's 'Big, Beautiful Door' Is a Big, Beautiful Step in the Right Direction," *Time*, October 29, 2015, http://time.com/4092571/republican-debate-immigration/.

37. Lauren Collins, "Can the Center Hold? Notes from a Free-for-All Election," Letter from France, *New Yorker*, May 8, 2017, 26.

38. A self-proclaimed "moderate" Le Pen supporter, the mayor of a small town, asked about "the well-dressed young immigrant men" in his town, "what are they doing *chez moi*?" Collins, "Can the Center Hold?," 24.

39. Again, this development moves freedom well beyond the scope and play imagined by the neoliberal intellectuals.

40. Even the extraordinarily careful and subtle Jacqueline Rose seems to flirt with the notion that these ugly impulses are just there, deep in the psyche, waiting to be activated or released. Rose, "Donald Trump's Victory Is a Disaster for Modern Masculinity." *Guardian*, November 15, 2016, https://www.theguardian.com/commentisfree/2016/nov/15/trump-disaster-modern-masculinity-sexual-nostalgian-oppressive-men-women.

41. The mantra, again, is freedom—freedom to do and say what one wants, grab what one can, and keep what one earns, freedom from the perceived requirement to check one's privilege and share the socioeconomic wealth. That entitlement was and is, of course, embodied by Donald Trump's own—not only his gilded bathtubs, his braggadocio about pussy grabbing, his "smart" tax avoidance, but his indignation after assuming office that he could not rule by fiat, fire the press, impose his Muslim ban, or in other ways vitiate the checks and balances that are the remains of liberal democracy.

42. Friedrich Nietzsche, *On the Genealogy of Morals*, trans. Walter Kaufmann (New York: Vintage, 1989), 75. "The struggle

against the Jews has always been a symptom of the worst charac-ters, those more envious and more cowardly. He who participates in it now must have much of the disposition of the mob." Nietzsche, quoted in Weaver Santaniello, "A Post-Holocaust Re-examination of Nietzsche and the Jews," in *Nietzsche and Jewish Culture*, ed. Jacob Golomb, 21–54 (London: Routledge, 1997).

43. Hans Sluga drew my attention to this in "Donald Trump: Between Populist Rhetoric and Plutocratic Rule," a paper presented at the UC Berkeley Critical Theory symposium on the election, February 2017. The paper is part of his larger work in progress on nihilism.

44. Sluga, "Donald Trump," 16; Friedrich Nietzsche, *The Will to Power*, trans. Walter Kaufmann (New York: Vintage, 1968), 9.

45. See Jack Edward Jackson, "Anti-Constitutionalism: Frontiers sans Frontiers," PhD diss., University of California, Berkeley, 2012. The revised dissertation is forthcoming as *Law without Future* (University of Pennsylvania Press, 2019).

46. Charles M. Blow, "Donald Trump: The Gateway Degenerate," *New York Times*, May 29, 2017, A21.

47. Nietzsche, *Will to Power*, 10.

48. Sluga, "Donald Trump," 16.

49. Sluga, "Donald Trump," 17

50. Sluga, "Donald Trump."

51. See Brown, *Undoing the Demos*, chap. 7.

52. Elizabeth Anker, "Ugly Freedoms," manuscript in progress.

53. Nietzsche, *Genealogy*, 67.

54. There are countless variations on this Trump voter's account of her support for him: "It doesn't seem like it makes any differ-ence which party gets in there. Whatever they say they'll do when they get in there, they can't really do it. . . . I just want him to annoy the hell out of everybody, and he's done that." Steven Rosenfeld, "Trump's Support Falling among Swing-State Voters Who Elected Him, Recent Polls Find," *Salon*, July 23, 2017, http://www.salon.com /2017/07/23/trumps-support-falling-among-swing-state-voters -who-elected-him-recent-polls-find_partner/?source=newsletter.

55. And, we need to add, when proletarianization shifts to the Global South, benefiting populations in the North with cheap and plentiful goods ranging from food and clothing to cars and electronics.

56. Herbert Marcuse, *One-Dimensional Man* (New York: Beacon, 1964), 76.

57. "Deprived of the claims which are irreconcilable with the established society, ... pleasure, thus adjusted, generates submission." Marcuse, *One-Dimensional Man*, 76.

58. Marcuse, *One-Dimensional Man*,

59. Marcuse, *One-Dimensional Man*,

60. Even as saying a strong "no" to the instincts or sublimating their energies into socially acceptable forms is supported and organized by prevailing social morality and theology and takes place at a largely unconscious level.

61. Marcuse describes an "atrophy of the mental organs for grasping the contradictions and the alternatives" and famously claims, "The real is rational ... and the established system delivers the goods." Marcuse, *One-Dimensional Man*, 79.

62. Marcuse, *One-Dimensional Man*, 77.

63. Marcuse, *One-Dimensional Man*, 77.

64. Marcuse, *One-Dimensional Man*, 79.

65. Marcuse, *One-Dimensional Man*, 78.

66. Marcuse, *One-Dimensional Man*, 78. Marcuse is departing here from Freud, who, in his later years, understood aggression to be weakened by a greater outlet for libidinal energies. For Marcuse, repressive desublimation involves what he calls a "compression" or concentration of erotic energy.

67. Marcuse, *One-Dimensional Man*,

68. Marcuse, *One-Dimensional Man*, 79.

THE AUTHORITARIAN PERSONALITY REVISITED

READING ADORNO IN THE AGE OF TRUMP

Peter E. Gordon

> Freud made the discovery—quite genuinely, simply through working on his own material—that the more deeply one explores the phenomena of human individuation, the more unreservedly one grasps the individual as a self-contained and dynamic entity, the closer one draws to that in the individual which is really no longer individual. THEODOR W. ADORNO, "INTRODUCTION TO SOCIOLOGY," 1968

> So many people are on television that don't know me, and they're like experts on me. DONALD J. TRUMP

In mid-January 2016, nearly a year before the inauguration of Donald J. Trump as the forty-fifth president of the United States, the online magazine *Politico* published a report with the title "One Weird Trait That Predicts Whether You're a Trump Supporter":

> If I asked you what most defines Donald Trump supporters, what would you say? They're white? They're poor? They're uneducated? You'd be wrong. In fact, I've found a single statistically significant

variable predicts whether a voter supports Trump—and it's not race, income or education levels: It's authoritarianism. That's right, Trump's electoral strength—and his staying power—have been buoyed, above all, by Americans with authoritarian inclinations. And because of the prevalence of authoritarians in the American electorate, among Democrats as well as Republicans, it's very possible that Trump's fan base will continue to grow.[1]

The author of this report, Matthew MacWilliams, is the founder of MacWilliams Sanders, a political communications firm, and he was also at the time a doctoral candidate in political science at the University of Massachusetts, Amherst, where he was writing his dissertation on authoritarianism.[2] Having conducted a national poll of eighteen hundred registered voters of varying political allegiance, MacWilliams reported that "education, income, gender, age, ideology and religiosity had no significant bearing on a Republican voter's preferred candidate." Edging out even "fear of terrorism," one statistical variable rose to the top as the distinguishing mark of a Donald Trump supporter: authoritarianism, which, MacWilliams noted, is "one of the most widely studied ideas" in the social sciences. Authoritarians, he explained, are inclined to "obey." They "rally to and follow strong leaders. And they respond aggressively to outsiders, especially when they feel threatened":

> Political pollsters have missed this key component of Trump's support because they simply don't include questions about authoritarianism in their polls. In addition to the typical battery of demographic, horse race, thermometer-scale and policy questions, my poll asked a set of four simple survey questions that political scientists have employed since 1992 to measure inclination toward authoritarianism. These questions pertain to child-rearing: whether it is more important for the voter to have a child who is respectful or independent; obedient or self-reliant; well-behaved or considerate; and well-mannered or curious. Respondents who pick the first option in each of these questions are strongly authoritar-

ian. Based on these questions, Trump was the only candidate—Republican or Democrat—whose support among authoritarians was statistically significant. It is time for those who would appeal to our better angels to take his insurgency seriously and stop dismissing his supporters as a small band of the dispossessed. Trump support is firmly rooted in American authoritarianism and, once awakened, it is a force to be reckoned with. That means it's also time for political pollsters to take authoritarianism seriously and begin measuring it in their polls.[3]

Although the tone of political urgency in the lines above may invite skepticism, we should still try to hear its distant echo of earlier research in social psychology spanning more than half a century. To grasp the implications of such research, it is crucial to recall the original aims of the landmark study published in 1950 as *The Authoritarian Personality*.[4] In what follows, I examine some of those aims, focusing on the study's premises and its possible missteps. I shall also consider Theodor Adorno's specific contributions, revisiting his written remarks, especially those that did not find their way into the published version of the study. My hope is that by reading Adorno again, we might discern how Trump both instantiates the category of the "authoritarian personality" and challenges its meaning. The *AP* study, I will suggest, developed two distinct lines of argument. The first of these, the "official" discovery of the research program, comprises the basic message that MacWilliams reiterates in the passages quoted above, namely, the claim to have identified a new "psychological type." The second argument is rather more sobering and radical in its implications: it suggests that the authoritarian personality signifies not merely a type but an emergent and generalized feature of modern society as such.

HISTORICAL AND THEORETICAL PREMISES

At the time Adorno and Max Horkheimer were first approached by the American Jewish Committee (AJC) to conduct research on anti-Semitism, the two men had just completed the initial draft of *Dialectic of Enlightenment*, the so-called philosophical fragments, in which they laid out a grandiose genealogy of instrumental reason spanning all of human history, from ancient myth to modern fascism. Composed in a highly abstract idiom, with literary readings of Homer's *Odyssey* and De Sade's *Juliette*, the *Dialectic* remained at a great remove from empirical commentary except perhaps for a damning chapter that examined the "culture industry" as the culminating phase in the liquidation of critical consciousness in modern society.[5] It is thus ironic that Adorno's biographer, Stefan Müller-Doohm, suggests we read *The Authoritarian Personality* as "a continuation of the *Dialectic of Enlightenment* by other means."[6] It is also worth noting that, through this study, both Adorno and Horkheimer came to a deepened admiration for the empiricist methods of the American social sciences. The truth of the matter, however, is that Adorno's collaboration with American social scientists exposed lines of tension that were never fully resolved.

Research for the study was a joint undertaking of the Institute for Social Research and the Public Opinion Study Group in Berkeley, California. In 1945, when the project was getting off the ground, Adorno was living in Los Angeles and would travel north every two weeks to San Francisco, to convene with his colleagues: Else Frenkel-Brunswik, a Polish-born refugee from Nazi Germany who had trained in Vienna as a psychoanalyst and served as a research associate in the Berkeley study; R. Nevitt Sanford, a Berkeley professor of psychology; and Daniel Levinson, at the time a research student at Berkeley and later a professor of psychology at Yale. The support from the AJC came at a moment of deep anxiety, especially for those who harbored personal fears regarding the possible resurgence of anti-Semitism in the United States, and we should not be surprised that these researchers brought to their task both a commitment to social scientific precision and a passionate belief in the necessity of defending the values of American democracy. Animating the study was the conviction that it should be possible to measure not just actively fascist commitment but fascism as a latent or explicit trait of consciousness. On the first page of the introduction, the authors explained:

> The research to be reported in this volume was guided by the following major hypothesis: that the political, economic, and social convictions of an individual often form a broad and coherent pattern, as if bound together by a "mentality" or "spirit," and that this pattern is an expression of deep-lying trends in his personality. The major concern was with the *potentially fascistic* individual, one whose structure is such as to render him particularly susceptible to anti-democratic propaganda.... [T]here was no difficulty in finding subjects whose outlook was such as to indicate that they would readily accept fascism if it should become a strong or respectable social movement.[7]

To measure this latent potential, the research team developed questionnaires that were distributed to a total of 2,099 subjects (mainly in the Bay Area, but also in Los Angeles, Oregon, and Washington, DC). The questionnaires were designed to map subject responses on four separate scales: the A-S scale (to measure anti-Semitism); the E scale (ethnocentrism); the PEC scale (politico-economic conservative ideological commitment, to distinguish genuine from so-called pseudoconservatives); and finally, the F scale (potential for fascism). This last metric was supposed to pick out a distinctive attitudinal structure called "authoritarianism," which consisted in nine characteristics:

a. *Conventionalism.* Rigid adherence to conventional, middle-class values.

b. *Authoritarian submission.* Submissive, uncritical attitude toward idealized moral authorities of the ingroup.

c. *Authoritarian aggression.* Tendency to be on the lookout for, and to condemn, reject, and punish people who violate conventional values.

d. *Anti-intraception.* Opposition to the subjective, the imaginative, the tender-minded.

   e. *Superstition and stereotypy.* The belief in mystical determinants of the individual's fate; disposition to think in rigid categories.

   f. *Power and "toughness."* Preoccupation with the dominance-submission, strong-weak, leader-follower dimension, identification with power-figures; overemphasis on conventionalized attributes of the ego; exaggerated assertion of strength and toughness.

   g. *Destructiveness and cynicism.* Generalized hostility; vilification of the human.

   h. *Projectivity.* The disposition to believe that wild and dangerous things go on in the world; projection outward of unconscious emotional impulses.

   i. *Sex.* Exaggerated concern with sexual "goings-on."[8]

"These variables," the authors wrote, "were thought of as going together to form a single syndrome, a more or less enduring structure in the person that renders him receptive to antidemocratic propaganda."[9] The assumption animating this study, in other words, that it should be possible to develop a profile of the sort of personality structure that would be predictive of high-scoring reports in terms of antidemocratic belief (ethnocentrism, anti-Semitism, and political-economic ideology) but without resorting in the questionnaires to explicit mention of these topics. The PEC scale was soon set aside, because its correlations with the E and A-S scales were not sufficiently high.[10] "What was needed," the researchers explained, "was a collection of items each of which was correlated with A-S and E but which did not come from an area ordinarily covered in discussions of political, economic, and social matters."[11] This would provide a portrait of latent characterological features that could, under certain circumstances, be awakened for fascist political ends. The F scale, the researchers explained, "attempts to measure the potentially antidemocratic personality."[12]

   The *AP* study represents one of the most significant attempts to correlate political ideology with psychoanalysis. But it was not the first venture by the Frankfurt School into empirical social psychology. Already in the 1920s, Erich Fromm had conducted empirical research on the political attitudes of the working class in Germany.[13] Then, in the mid-1930s, borrowing from Sigmund Freud and especially from the "character-analysis" of Wilhelm Reich, Fromm collaborated with Herbert Marcuse and Horkheimer on *Studies on Authority and the Family*, laying bare a psychoanalytically inflected portrait of the "sado-masochistic character" prone to fascism.[14] Such studies drew their energy from the frustrated hope of a historical materialism that had expected a natural alliance between the working class and revolutionary consciousness. The scandal of a working class that moved against its own ostensibly objective interests could only be made intelligible by measuring the depths of subjective consciousness and reaching for the language of psychopathology. All of these studies moved in the dialectical space between sociology and psychoanalysis, guided by the critical ambition that one might develop, without reductionism, a correlation between objective socioeconomic conditions and subjective features of individual personality.[15] But sustaining a genuinely dialectical understanding of the relation between the psychological and the social clearly remained a great challenge. As later critics would observe, the *AP* authors seemed to commit an unwarranted reification of consciousness when they announced in the book's opening pages that they had identified nothing less than a new "anthropological species" or "authoritarian type."[16]

In the book's foreword, coauthored by Horkheimer and Samuel H. Flowerman (the codirectors of the broader series Studies in Prejudice, sponsored by the AJC), one can already detect a certain embarrassment regarding the dominance of individual consciousness as an independent variable. "It may strike the reader," they wrote,

that we have placed undue stress on the personal and the psychological rather than upon the social aspect of prejudice. This is not due to a personal preference for psychological analysis nor to a failure to see that the cause of irrational hostility is in the last instance to be found in social frustration and injustice. Our aim is not merely to describe prejudice but to explain it in order to help in its eradication. . . . Eradication means re-education. And education in a strict sense is by its nature personal and psychological.[17]

Even if it could be justified by practical aims, they argued, the emphasis on individual psychology would need to be supplemented by research into the social and historical conditions to explain both the emergence and the prevalence of the new anthropological type. Although the present studies were "essentially psychological in nature," Horkheimer and Flowerman acknowledged that one had to explain all individual behavior "in terms of social antecedents." "The individual in vacuo," they declared, "is but an artifact."[18]

And yet it seems fair to say that the very notion of an authoritarian personality or character worked against sociological explanation, discouraging an account of individual human psychology as a social artifact. Instead of enforcing a dialectical image of the relation between the psychological and the social, it tended to reify the psychological as the antecedent condition, thereby diminishing what was for critical theory a sine qua non for all interdisciplinary labor joining sociology to psychoanalysis. The recent work by MacWilliams (which reflects formidable research effort and should not be lightly dismissed) would appear to reflect this understanding of psychology as the prior explanatory variable, given the way it tries to isolate "authoritarianism," as if it were a stable category for sociological analysis prior to other affiliations or identifying social factors. This is not to fault MacWilliams himself, who in this respect is surely confronting one of the most challenging dilemmas in the human sciences, traceable as far back as the nineteenth-century studies in moral statistics and Emile Durkheim's efforts to correlate even the most interior distress of suicide with sociological trends. MacWilliams is hardly alone in following this line of research, and he is unlikely to be the last. As Thomas Wheatland notes, *The Authoritarian Personality* "enjoyed a major impact on the history of sociology."[19] Within five years of its publication in 1950, it had inspired at least sixty-four related studies and a host of commentary. The Dutch sociologist Jos Meloen notes that over four decades, from 1950 to 1990, *Psychological Abstracts* listed more than *two thousand* published studies on authoritarianism, and citations to the original study the research group identified as "Adorno et al." also soared beyond two thousand.[20]

To be sure, the *AP* study has never lacked for detractors. Especially during the Cold War, it faced fierce criticism in part because of the Frankfurt School affiliations of the larger Studies in Prejudice research program. Critics such as the University of Chicago sociologist Edward Shils charged the authors with political bias for failing to acknowledge the possibility of "left-wing authoritarianism."[21] Such accusations assumed a more ominous tone when McCarthyism descended upon the Berkeley faculty, and R. Nevitt Sanford, one of the original *AP* authors, was dismissed for his refusal to sign the loyalty oath. (Together with forty-five other nonsigners, Sanford brought the case to court; he was reinstated to his post by the end of 1952.) Others have criticized the study on methodological grounds. The Rutgers sociologist John Levi Martin has called it "probably the most deeply flawed work of prominence in political psychology."[22] Its fatal error, in his opinion, lay in marrying nominalist research procedures (based on the quantified empirical ranking of responses) with a realist specification of types (based on the a priori belief that human psychology divides up into distinct profiles). The essential charge is that of confirmation bias, that the research team knew in advance what they were looking for and devised the questionnaires only to pick out the relevant psychological types. Despite ongoing controversies over its legitimacy, however, the original study merits our attention especially today, when the spectacle of American politics invites anxious comparison to the political trends of an earlier age. The question that deserves our consideration is whether the political problems now looming before us in the United States permit us to mobilize concepts first developed in the *AP* study, and whether Adorno's own contributions to that study retain any explanatory power after more than half a century.

ADORNO'S ROLE IN THE *AUTHORITARIAN PERSONALITY* STUDY

When confronted with the findings of an empirical research program, the facile conclusion for the critical theorist is to invoke the half-imagined specter of American positivism, as if this were sufficient to dismiss any partnership with the qualitative and quantitative social sciences. In fact, Adorno enjoyed himself during his collaboration with the Berkeley psychologists, and many years later, in 1986, Sanford wrote in a brief comment on the early study that "Adorno was a most stimulating intellectual companion. He had what seemed to us a profound grasp of psychoanalytic theory, complete familiarity with the ins and outs of German fascism and, not least, a boundless supply of off-color jokes." Less humorously, but theoretically of greater import, Sanford explained that Adorno

> was very helpful when it came to thinking up items for the F scale. More than that... his joining our staff "led to an expansion and deepening of our work." It may well have been under the influence of Adorno that I wrote in the concluding chapter of AP: "The modification of the potentially fascist structure cannot be achieved by psychological means alone. The task is comparable to that of eliminating neurosis, or delinquency, or nationalism from the world. These are products of the total organization of society and are to be changed only as that society is changed."[23]

Sanford's favorable memories of collaboration with Adorno qualify the sometimes exaggerated image of the Frankfurt School theorists as unrepentant mandarins who suffered during their American exile in a state of intellectual isolation.[24] Further contradicting this impression, we have Adorno's own letter to Horkheimer, written in November 1944 when he had first joined the Berkeley group and was helping craft the F scale by drawing upon the anti-Semitism chapter from *Dialectic of Enlightenment*. "I have distilled a number of questions by means of a kind of translation from the 'Elements of Anti-Semitism,'" Adorno wrote, adding, "It was all a lot of fun."[25]

Just how Adorno found amusement in this effort is something that may deserve more scrutiny. But rather than dwell on this point, I will suggest that we focus our attention on a different sort of problem that afflicted the *AP* study without ever coming into sharp relief. The problem is whether it is plausible to identify something like a "personality" at all. Needless to say, this is distinct from the classical question of sociological or psychological reduction, or whether, in the relation between sociological and psychological conditions, either should be granted greater explanatory force. Sanford himself acknowledged that it was Adorno who encouraged him to see the phenomenon of the authoritarian personality within the dialectical matrix of sociological conditions. But even here Sanford omits a deeper and more challenging theoretical question as to the status of individual psychology. To bring this theoretical question into view, we must direct our attention to an unintended irony that ran through the entire study from beginning to end.

Although *The Authoritarian Personality* was a multiauthor work, individual chapters were assigned to different members in the research group. Adorno himself wrote chapter 19, which bears the title "Types and Syndromes." The following passage in particular warrants further scrutiny:

> Our typology has to be a *critical* typology in the sense that it comprehends the typification of men itself as a social function. The more rigid a type, the more deeply does he show the hallmarks of

social rubber stamps. This is in accordance with the characterization of our high scorer by traits such as rigidity and stereotypical
thinking. Here lies the ultimate principle of our whole typology.
Its major dichotomy lies in the question of whether a person is stan-
dardized himself and thinks in a standardized way, or whether he is
truly "individualized" and opposes standardization in the sphere of
human experience. The individual types will be specific configura-
tions within this general division. The latter differentiates *prima*
facie between high and low scorers. At closer view, however, it also
affects the low scorers themselves: the more they are "typified"
themselves, the more they express unwittingly the fascist potential within themselves.[26]

Here a certain irony comes into view, even if it remains only par-
tially recognized and thematically underdeveloped. In Adorno's
suggestion—that a given person may be "standardized" and
"think" in a standardized way or may instead "oppose" standardization—we may detect a self-reflexivity problem. The distinction risks measuring the high-scoring subject on the F scale
against a triumphalist image of the true individual who is apparently immune to typological thinking. Only the "high-scoring"
individual is prone to stereotypical thinking. The distinction
itself, in other words, looks at social reality from the perspective of the high-scoring subject rather than the true individual.
This opens up the possibility of a vicious circle or self-referential
paradox where the principle that animates the study becomes
trapped in its own diagnostic. If stereotypical thinking involves
the reduction of differentiated persons to quasi-natural kinds,
one cannot help but wonder if the social-psychological method
of the study itself has not deployed the very technique it marks
as a pathology.

To rescue the research study from this self-referential problem, we need to recognize that (from Adorno's perspective) the
very category of a "true individual" was beginning to vanish from
social reality. This rather sobering suggestion makes only an in-

termittent appearance in the published study; it comes most to
the fore as a defense against the criticism that the study had produced a set of reified psychological types. It should not surprise
us that even these suggestions appear only in the "Types and
Syndromes" chapter authored by Adorno. "The critique of typology," he writes, "should not neglect the fact that large numbers
of people are no longer, or rather never were, 'individuals' in
the sense of traditional nineteenth-century philosophy." What
appeared to be a flaw in the research method could be described
as a flaw in the social order itself: "There is reason to look for psychological types," Adorno explains, "*because the world in which we
live is typed and 'produces' different 'types' of persons.*"[27]

For Adorno, then, it was misleading to identify a new "anthropological type" alongside others that could be ranked on a
scale of differing styles of psychology or "character" (the latter
being the term Adorno preferred). After all, the drive to identify
psychological types was *itself* a symptom of typological thinking
and therefore betrayed the very same penchant for standardization that it claimed to criticize in social reality. At the same
time, however, such a research agenda corresponded to emergent patterns in contemporary social reality. Modern patterns
of economic exchange and commoditized cultural experience
meant that genuine individuals were gradually being reduced to
social types, and this developing feature of society itself served as
a realist justification for a research agenda that methodologically
compressed individuals into recognizable social types. Lurking in
this argument, however, was a far more radical claim that identified stereotypical thinking and authoritarianism with general
features of the modern social order itself. This is the largely un-
stated implication of Adorno's phrase "The world in which we
live is typed." This crucial suggestion, however, remains barely
legible in the published version of *The Authoritarian Personality*, chiefly because the official study represented a compromise
between various legitimate, if competing, research agendas. The
social psychologists who collaborated with Adorno were clearly

less inclined to accept the historicized and sociological metamorphosis of psychoanalytic doctrine that Adorno and Horkheimer had developed as representatives of the European and Marxist-oriented tradition of critical theory. Nor could the "practical" and democratic-educative purposes of the *AP* study (written in the American context and imprinted with an American spirit of social possibility) easily accommodate the rather grim if not totalizing indictment of modernity that had become by this stage a principled theoretical stance for the two coauthors of *Dialectic of Enlightenment*.

The disparity of opinion between the AJC and the Frankfurt School becomes evident if we consult the private letter that Horkheimer sent to Marcuse on July 17, 1943, *well before* the Berkeley research project had commenced:

> The problem of Antisemitism is much more complicated than I thought in the beginning. *I don't have to tell you that I don't believe in psychology as in a means to solve a problem of such seriousness.* I did not change a bit my skepticism towards that discipline. Also, the term psychology as I use it in the project stands for anthropology and anthropology for the theory of man as he has developed under the conditions of antagonistic society. It is my intention to study the presence of the scheme of domination in the so-called psychological life, the instincts as well as the thoughts of men. The tendencies in people which make them susceptible to propaganda for terror are themselves the result of terror, physical and spiritual, actual and potential oppression. If we could succeed in describing the patterns, according to which domination operates even in the remotest domains of the mind, we would have done a worthwhile job. But to achieve this one must study a great deal of the silly psychological literature and if you could see my notes... you would probably think I have gone crazy myself.[28]

Such complaints suggest that Horkheimer, like Adorno, must have moderated many of his more radical opinions so as to achieve some measure of comity with his American colleagues. There remained a marked disagreement between the researchers' thesis of a distinctively authoritarian "type" and the Frankfurt School's more global indictment of modern society.

ADORNO'S UNPUBLISHED "REMARKS"

These more global implications are best understood if one consults "Remarks on *The Authoritarian Personality*," a brief theoretical essay, still unpublished, that Adorno originally meant to include in the published volume. We have no recorded explanation as to why "Remarks" did not appear in the finished text, but the likely answer becomes apparent once we examine its content. On the very first page Adorno takes care to emphasize the problem of prior sociological conditioning. "Our probing into prejudice is devoted to subjective aspects," he explains:

> We are not analyzing objective social forces which produce and reproduce bigotry, such as economic and historical determinants. Even short-term factors like propaganda do not enter into the picture per se, though a number of major hypotheses stem from propaganda analyses carried out by the Institute of Social Research. All the stimuli enhancing prejudice, and even the entire cultural climate—imbued with minority stereotypes as it is—are regarded as presuppositions. Their effect upon our subjects is not followed up; we remain, so to say, in the realm of "reactions," not of stimuli.[29]

Needless to say, this was a remarkable statement of methodological dissent, as it suggests a far more generalized indictment of pathologies that afflict not only individuals but what Adorno called the "entire cultural climate." According to this line of analysis, social psychology could hardly suffice as a research method if it contented itself with the mere aggregation of individualized psychological profiles, when the general trend of social standardization was actually weakening the individual psyche. "We are convinced," Adorno explained, "that the ultimate source of prejudice has to be sought in social factors which are incomparably stronger than the 'psyche' of any one individual involved. This assumption is corroborated by the results of the study itself, insofar as it shows that conformity to values implicitly promoted by the 'objective spirit' of today's American society is one of the major traits of our high-scoring subjects."[30] Resisting the temptation of isolating a distinctively authoritarian personality, Adorno concludes that anti-Semitism, fascism, and authoritarianism are due to "the total structure of our society."[31]

Such criticism regarding the "objective spirit" of the contemporary United States may have reflected Adorno's personal sense of alienation as a European in exile. But we cannot dismiss his remarks as mere reflexes of biography or signs of cultural elitism. Rather, they identify a far-reaching methodological critique of what he calls the "democratic bias" in quantified social-scientific inquiry, in which validity becomes little more than a precipitate of mass opinion. The correlation between subjective patterns of belief and objective features of the social order, in other words, cannot be derived reductively through the aggregation of subjective mentality without reproducing the subjectivist ideology of the market economy itself, in which the success of a commodity is said to derive from nothing more than the quantified individual desires of the consumer:

> Thus we fully realize that limiting the study to subjective aspects is not without its dangers. Our detailed analysis of subjective patterns does not mean that, in our opinion, prejudice can be explained in such terms. On the contrary, we regard the analysis of objective social forces which engender prejudice as the most pressing issue in contemporary research into anti-minority bias. The relative negligence with which this task is treated throughout American research is due to its "democratic bias," to the idea that socially valid scientific findings can be gained only by sampling a

vast number of people on whose opinions and attitudes depends what is going to happen—just as success or failure of a commodity offered on the market supposedly depends on the mentality of the buyer.[32]

For Adorno, then, the individualistic or "democratic" strategy of aggregative social research reproduces a fetishistic understanding of society as the aggregate of subjective opinion, a correlation that would hold only if society were actually composed of substantive "individuals." But Adorno challenges precisely this premise as ideological, corresponding to a historical phase that has been surpassed. In his analysis, the "high-scoring" individual appears less as a case of social pathology than as an emergent social norm:

> Methodologically, a not insignificant result of our study is the suspicion that the aforementioned assumption does no longer hold true. Our high-scoring subjects do not seem to behave as autonomous units whose decisions are important for their own fate as well as that of society, but rather as submissive centers of reactions, looking for the conventional "thing to do," and riding what they consider "the wave of the future." This observation seems to fall in line with the economic tendency towards gradual disappearance of the free market and the adaptation of man to the slowly emerging new condition. Research following the conventional patterns of investigation into public opinion may easily reach the point where the orthodox concept of what people feel, want, and do proves to be obsolete.[33]

For Adorno, the high-scoring subjects could no longer be dismissed as exceptional. Rather, they became *paradigmatic* or intensified instances of trends that were increasingly visible across the whole of modern society. In this sense, they were more "true" than the true individuals whose low scores implied a greater capacity to resist the allures of fascist propaganda. "As far as the timeliness of 'highs' and 'lows' is concerned," Adorno wrote, "our finding that the 'highs' conform more thoroughly to the prevailing cultural climate and are—at least superficially—better adjusted than the 'lows,' seems to indicate that, measured by standards of the status quo, they are also more characteristic of the present historical situation."[34]

Such remarks were clearly more radical in their implications than the AP research program could allow. For if the concept of "what people feel, want, and do" had lost its traction as a descriptive instrument for individual-psychological phenomena, this was the case only because the object it meant to describe—the individual psyche—was itself beginning to dissolve. Ironically, this objective dissolution of the strong or bourgeois "self" suggested that psychoanalysis too was beginning to lose its salience, while the behaviorist's reductive model of the self as a mere "bundle of reflexes" was assuming the status of objective truth. "It may be a function of our study," Adorno observes, "to point out the limitations of psychological determinants in modern man and their replacement by omnipotent social adjustment, which, psychologically viewed, is retrogressive, and, at the same time, comes close to the behaviorists' concept of man as a bundle of conditioned reflexes."[35]

The general trend of society was "retrogressive," moving away from genuine individuality and toward an increase in social behavior that the AP study identified with "high" scores. "Today," Adorno explains, "men tend to become transformed into 'social agencies' and to lose the qualities of independence and resistance which used to define the old concept of the individual. The traditional dichotomy between objective social forces and individuals, which we maintain methodologically, thus loses some of its substance."[36] The dissolution of the older, psychoanalytic model of the self under the pressure of social standardization thus implied an undialectical fusion between subject and object—between psyche and society—a trend that seemed to confirm Adorno and Horkheimer's broader thesis regarding the rise of an "affirmative" social order, in which individual resistance had become virtually impossible. "We may at least venture the hypothesis," Adorno observed, "that the psychology of the contemporary anti-semite in a way presupposes the end of psychology itself."[37]

It should not surprise us that the collaborative research team did not include these remarks in the published text of *The Authoritarian Personality*. For if Adorno was right, then the very notion of individual psychology had to be treated with the deepest skepticism. Even psychoanalysis in his view promoted the model of an integrated and separable personality, but while this expressed the sociological truth of the nineteenth-century bourgeoisie, it was no longer adequate for understanding the dynamics of a fully integrated modern social order. In this respect, even psychoanalysis was objectively false and, in cleaving to a model of autonomous depth, ideological in the technical sense. The low-scoring individual on the F scale was therefore for Adorno a kind of remnant of a society verging on disappearance. The penchant for stereotyping that was ostensibly an affliction of a distinctively authoritarian personality was in fact due to the stereotyping of consciousness that in modern society had become the social norm. It was this far more general characterization that moved Adorno to declare, "People are inevitably as irrational as the world in which they live."[38] Even if psychoanalysis still held up to society the unrealized ideal of an autonomous individual, the power of the culture industry and the stereotyping of everyday life made this ideal increasingly marginal, if not a kind of utopian impossibility. As the power of society intruded upon the individual, the very paranoia of authoritarianism expressed, though without critical awareness, a truth about current social conditions that was in a way far more accurate than the psychoanalytic ideal. It was Leo Löwenthal who observed that mass culture was "psychoanalysis in reverse."[39] For Adorno, this reversal was not isolated to an authoritarian personality; it had become a generalized sociological fact. This argument implies a dialectical overcoming of the *AP* research agenda, pressing beyond even the interdisciplinary communion of sociology and psychology toward an indictment of the very premises of psychology itself.

PSYCHOANALYSIS AND FASCIST PROPAGANDA

Adorno's grim perspective on the prospects for social psychology may explain why the "Remarks" were not included in the published 1950 text of *The Authoritarian Personality*. But it may also deepen our appreciation for an essay Adorno published just a year later, in the volume *Psychoanalysis and the Social Sciences*, under the title "Freudian Theory and the Pattern of Fascist Propaganda." Here Adorno states emphatically, and in apparent contradiction to the *AP* study, that "fascism as such is *not* a psychological issue."[40] For "only an explicit theory of society, by far transcending the range of psychology, can fully answer the question raised here [regarding fascism's group-psychological efficacy]."[41] The essay indeed reads as if it were meant to *revoke* the strongly psychological interpretation of fascism to which he had so recently contributed. Its internal dialogue with the *AP* study becomes most apparent when Adorno explains that fascism "relies absolutely on the total structure as well as on each particular trait of *the authoritarian character which is itself the product of an internalization of the irrational aspects of modern society.*"[42] For Adorno, the theory of fascism put forward by the *AP* study had mistakenly reversed the directionality of causation. Rather than affirming the authoritarian personality as the *source* of fascism's appeal, Adorno insisted that an authoritarian "character" be seen as the *introjection* of an irrational society. "Psychological dispositions do not actually cause fascism," Adorno explained. "Rather, fascism defines a psychological area which can be successfully exploited by the forces which promote it for entirely nonpsychological reasons of self-interest."[43]

Yet, notwithstanding this apparent disavowal of psychological causation, we find in this essay some of Adorno's more prescient insights regarding the psychological techniques and experiences that serve to mobilize or inspire the fascist crowd. Most pertinent is his insight, following Freud, into the strange sense of artifice and theatricality that undercuts any liberal theory of mass "barbarism." It is not that fascism is somehow uncivilized or a symptom of genuine regression. Rather, in the rallies and speeches that serve as the crucial vehicles of fascist propaganda, spectators partake in an illusion of barbarism. They experience the *fantasy* of their own regression to a state of uncivilized or desublimated ecstasy, while at the same time recognizing this regression as little more than a performance. Borrowing from Freud's analysis of group psychology, Adorno characterizes this phenomenon as an "*artificial regression*":[44]

> The category of "phoniness" applies to the leaders as well as to the act of identification on the part of the masses and their supposed frenzy and hysteria. Just as little as people believe in the depth of their hearts that the Jews are the devil, do they completely believe in the leader. They do not really identify themselves with him but act this identification, perform their own enthusiasm, and thus participate in their leader's performance. It is through this performance that they strike a balance between their continuously mobilized instinctual urges and the historical stage of enlightenment they have reached, and which cannot be revoked arbitrarily.[45]

Adorno ascribes a singular importance to this phenomenon of narcissistic identification. The fascist leader appears to his followers as an "enlargement of the subject's own personality."[46] This identification reveals an apparent paradox, in that the leader's claim to authority is grounded not in love but only in the primitive mechanisms of fear and hatred. Because the leader lacks a "positive program," his leadership draws its power less from a substantive vision of the future than from "threat and denial." In Adorno words, "the leader can be loved only if he himself does not love."[47] The collective reveals its own lack of identity: it understands itself only by means of a negative fantasy about those who are excluded or whom it wishes to exclude. Hostility becomes the very medium of social solidarity, and "greatness" means little more than building a wall.

But on this point we should read Adorno's analysis with great care: Adorno is not suggesting that the psychological mechanism of identification lay at the root of fascism's success. On the contrary, he urges us to see that this identification itself is a kind of performance or simulacrum of a psychological bond. Notice Adorno's remark in the passage above that the "phoniness" *applies to the act of identification* itself. That this identification is mere artifice should be obvious from the fact that the fascist leader wields a privileged power wholly unlike the crowd that longs for identification:

> Even the fascist leader's startling symptoms of inferiority, his resemblance to ham actors and asocial psychopaths, is . . . anticipated in Freud's theory. For the sake of those parts of the follower's narcissistic libido that have not been thrown into the leader image but remain attached to the follower's own ego, the superman must still resemble the follower and appear as his "enlargement." Accordingly, one of the basic devices of personalized fascist propaganda is the concept of the "great little man," a person who suggests both omnipotence and the idea that he is just one of the folks, a plain, red-blooded American, untainted by material or spiritual wealth. Psychological ambivalence helps to work a social miracle. The leader image gratifies the follower's twofold wish to submit to authority and to be the authority himself.[48]

In this analysis, fascism becomes simultaneously truth *and* untruth: On the one hand, it holds out to the masses the promise of a collective release from the constraints of bourgeois civilization with its demand that all instinct (and perhaps especially violence) submit to a pathological repression. Condemning this repression as pathological, it presents itself as the "honest" or "forthright" acknowledgment of everything one is not supposed to say or do. On the other hand, it offers merely the *performance* of this release, through the fantasy of identification with a leader who offers *both* the experience of masochistic submission *and* the illusion that he is just like his followers. This is fascism's "social miracle," which, like all miracles, serves as a dream of redemption without providing any actual transformation from the social conditions of unhappiness. Fascism thus promotes "identification with the existent," a strategy that aligns it (as Adorno explains elsewhere) with the ideological underpinnings of Heidegger's philosophy. The artifice of this identification, incidentally, is not unlike the artifice that Adorno discerns in Heidegger's "jargon of authenticity," in which the philosophical language that promises to restore wholeness to the fallen world turns out to be indistinguishable from the language of modern advertising.[49]

DJT; OR, THE CULTURE INDUSTRY AS POLITICS

I have explored, in this essay, some of the complications in the notion of an "authoritarian personality." More specifically, I have laid out ways in which Adorno dissented from the official thesis of the 1950 research program. Throughout this exposition, I have aimed to recover, chiefly through indirection, themes in Adorno's analysis that may have some bearing on our interpretation of current political phenomena in the United States. In particular, I have tried to suggest that the notion of an "authoritarian personality" may not prove adequate. For what Adorno was identifying in fascism was not a structure of psychology or the political precipitate of a psychological disposition. Rather, it was a generalized feature of the social order itself. Trumpism, if we can call it that, is far more than Donald Trump, and perhaps also far less than the specter of "fascism" sometimes invoked anxiously by his political critics. If Adorno was right, if his initial insights still obtain, we might conclude as follows.

Trumpism is not anchored in a specific species of personality that can be distinguished from other personalities and placed on a scale from which the critic with an ostensibly healthy psychology is somehow immune. Nor is it confined to the right-wing fringe of the Republican Party, so that those who self-identify with the left might congratulate themselves as not being responsible for its creation. Nor can it be explained as the Frankenstein's monster of a racism once deployed cynically as a dog whistle by both the Republican and Democratic Parties, and now expressed openly, without embarrassment, with plainspoken American candor. Most of all, Trumpism is not the mere upsurge of an angry populism that has taken elites by surprise. We have difficulty recognizing this inconvenient and unsettling fact, that much of Trump's appeal was utterly *unexceptional*. Those on the left who cling as a matter of principle to socioeconomic explanations often prefer to interpret Trumpism as a kind of misplaced "protest" against the inequities of global capitalism, but in doing so they neglect an overwhelming statistical truth, that the greatest share of Trump voters were not disaffected members of the downwardly mobile white working class but lifetime Republicans, members of the broad and suburban American middle classes who voted for Trump simply because he was the Republican candidate. Trumpism is not a social pathology but another instance of the general pathology that is American political culture.

Trumpism is sufficiently complex as to overwhelm any single framework of analysis. Theories that see it as a departure from the norm may explain some aspects of the phenomenon, and each may hold a special appeal in some precinct of criticism. Trumpism holds a powerful fascination for its critics precisely because it serves as an object for our negative self-definition. For his admiring crowds, Trump is refreshing precisely for his ineloquence, for his swagger, for allusions to violence that typically remain at the level of tough talk but at times spill over into real action. For his opponents, however, Trump seems to occasion a kind of hypereloquence, as if one could perform through language the mind's distance from mindlessness. For whatever it is, Trumpism is not *us*, and that is its hidden consolation. This is the moment of dishonesty in political criticism, that it forges a negative cathexis against the enemy who permits us better to define who we are. Trump is indeed entertainment but not only for those whom it entertains. If Trump enchants his supporters, he awakens a no less powerful fascination for the critics who loathe him, since love and loathing are only two sides of the same coin.

The real importance in Adorno's criticism, I would suggest, is the fact that he refused to identify such social pathologies with specific personalities or social groups. Adorno had already glimpsed the emergence of a social order that would do away with the consolation of the "scale," which places the critic at the furthest remove from the object of criticism; in his view, all of society was marked with the pathology its liberal critics would reserve only for others. Trumpism, masquerading as society's rebellion against its own unfreedom, represents not an actual rebellion but the standardization of rebellion and the saturation of consciousness by media forms.

If Adorno was right, then Trumpism cannot be interpreted as an instance of a personality or a psychology, but must be recognized as the thoughtlessness of the entire culture. It is a thoughtlessness and a penchant for standardization that today marks not just Trump and his followers but nearly all forms of culture, and nearly all forms of discourse. The eclipse of serious journalism by punchy sound bites and outraged tweets, and the polarized, standardized reflection of opinion into forms of humor and theatricalized outrage within narrow niche markets, makes the category of individual thought increasingly unreal. This is true on the left as well as the right, and it is especially noteworthy once we countenance what passes for political discourse today. Instead of a public sphere, we have what Jürgen Habermas long ago called the refeudalization of society and the mere performance of publicity *before* an abject public that has grown accustomed to inaction. The new media forms have devolved into entertainment; instead of critical discourse we see the spectacle of a commentariat, across the ideological spectrum, that prefers outrage to complexity and dismisses dialectical uncertainty for the narcissistic affirmation of self-consistent ideologies, each parceled out via its own private cable network. Expression is displacing critique. It should astonish us more than it does that so many people now confess to learning about the news through comedy shows, where audiences can experience their convictions only with an ironist's laughter. A strange phenomenon of half-belief has seized consciousness, as if ignorance were tinged with both knowingness and shame, the implicit recognition that, in identifying with a political ideology, actual criticism yields to mere thoughtlessness. A genuinely *critical* public sphere would involve argument rather than irony. But publicity today has shattered into a series of niche markets within which one swoons to one's preferred slogan and already knows what one knows. Name just about any political position and what sociologists call "pillarization"—or what the Frankfurt School called "ticket" thinking—will predict, almost without fail, a full suite of opinions. This is as true for enthusiasts in the Democratic Party as for those who support Trump. The phenomenon of standardization through the mass media signifies not the return of fascism but the dissolution of critical consciousness itself, and it heralds the slow emergence of something rather different than political struggle: the mediatized enactment of politics in quotation marks, where all political substance is slowly being drained away.

This, I think, is why the phenomenon of Trumpism remains so difficult to comprehend. As Adorno recognized long ago, there is a kind of artifice to this rebellion that belongs less to what we used to call political reality than it does to reality television. It is true that Trump says outrageous things and, as his champions often say, "tells it like it is." But the strange aspect to this candor is that one cannot get over the impression that he hardly means what he says. He is as likely to reverse his opinion in the next moment and to deny what he has just said. Those who support him say one shouldn't take offense, that this is just Trump being Trump.

When he "tells it like it is," the authenticity of his performance is precisely the *performance of authenticity*. With the casual bluster of a talk-radio host, attitude displaces meaning, and the telling displaces what is told. Trump constantly invokes "political correctness" as an evil force of liberal repression, and it is therefore tempting to consider him a kind of impresario for what liberalism has repressed. But Trumpism is less the "undoing" of repression than it is an event of political theater, in which everyone gets to experience the *apparent* dismantling of repression without anything actually changing. Even his unabashed misogyny, racism, and demagogic remarks about Muslims merely recapitulate a repertoire of stereotyped attitudes that have long characterized American public discourse. In his campaign rallies, in his public speeches as president, and in the absurdly abbreviated form of his compulsive "tweets," he seems to recycle a stream of clichés that bear an uncanny resemblance to the language of the playground: Hillary Clinton becomes "crooked Hillary," Africans live in "huts," and Kim Jong-un, the supreme leader of North Korea, becomes "little rocket man." Although "crooked" is an archaic term in English that evokes the morally impoverished landscape of fairy tales, the media dutifully reports such rubbish as newsworthy. In its hunger for the latest scandal the media thereby succumbs to the same game of pseudoregression, where even affairs of state are reduced to childish theatrics. The point here is that Trumpism is a scandal—but not because it represents a departure from the otherwise healthy and mature norms of American democracy. Too easily condemned as exceptional, the vulgarity and simplicity that has become Trump's trademark style is not exceptional at all: it is a symptom of a culture that has succumbed to the thoughtlessness of received typologies. Hence the importance of Adorno's remark that the authoritarian personality represents, not a pathology from which some can claim immunity, but "the total structure of our society."[50] If Trumpism seems to belie the research categories of *The Authoritarian Personality*, we might do better to turn to the Frankfurt School's analysis of the culture industry. Trumpism itself, one could argue, is just another name for the culture industry, where the performance of undoing repression serves as a means for carrying on precisely as before.

Now, if one were to ask how this apotheosis of the culture industry occurred, we would have to admit that its patterns appear well before our current age. It was anticipated in 1960, in the televised Nixon-Kennedy debates, where performance mattered as much as ideology; it was anticipated in the 1980s, in the strange apparition of Ronald Reagan, whose habit of quoting lines from his own Hollywood films helped keep alive a fantasy of a vanished America.[51] Contemporary American society has taken up this habit of repetition with a vengeance. Video screens are now pervasive in our daily lives, not only in our homes, but in stores, airports, at the gas pump and, of course, in our own hands. The strategy of "message-testing" through focus groups has become as omnipresent and obligatory a feature of mass politics as it is of mass-produced music, turning political campaigns into exercises in the engineering of slogans, which crowds shout back in unison as if repeating the chorus of a popular song.[52] The evacuation of content from politics and the emergence of a desubstantialized and mediatized performance of political forms is not really new. But it has now reached such a point of extremity that we should hardly be surprised when a man who owes most of his seeming reality to "reality television" manages to triumph over the gray eminences of "real" political experience. Trumpism is politics in quotation marks, but ours is an age in which the quotation mark has reshaped not only political experience but experience as such.

This sense of artifice is especially noteworthy in the case of Trump, whose improbable victory in the United States presidential elections of November 2016 seems more like an episode in "reality television" than the fulfillment of a distinctive ideological agenda. If one is seeking a psychological etiology, incompetence, megalomania, and a longing to bask in the glow of the media may go further toward explaining his unexpected election than alarmist attempts to characterize it as fascism's second coming. It is true, of course, that during his first year in office Trump surrounded himself with ideologues such as Steven Bannon and Sebastian Gorka, who represent the genuinely hateful forces of the radical, or "alt," right. Bannon, for one, even expressed admiration for Julius Evola, one of the more notorious pseudophilosophers in the pantheon of Italian fascism. But Trump himself remains an ideological enigma. Lurching from crisis to crisis, his unsteady leadership has produced a great many spectacles for media consumption, but it has not yet produced much coherence in policy. Crowding about him like courtiers at Versailles are enthusiasts for a multitude of conflicting interest groups— Christian evangelicals and libertarians, neonationalists and neoconservatives, populist advocates of the disenfranchised white working class, and well-heeled representatives of the Republican establishment—all of them competing for the President's attention but none of them confident they can hold it for long. At the center of this chaos lies a kind of ideological vacuum: the man who once identified as a Democrat and now identifies as a Republican may in fact be little more than a chameleon, driven not primarily by ideology but by a narcissistic longing for approval. He's seemed happiest at the mass rallies he continues to hold even as president where he can indulge his taste for theatrics and encourage adoring crowds to chant back to him the slogans that became the trademarks of his campaign. If there is a driving purpose in all this disorder it is the paradigmatic opportunism of the American businessman or con artist who only wants to close the sale. While Trump has never sold snake-oil, he did once sell steak, and during a March 2016 news conference even promised his brand-name meats as gifts to political supporters.[53] Whatever his ideological agenda or his personal motivations, his victory ultimately signifies an emptiness at the core of American commercial culture. Little in the character or "personality" of this insubstantial man suggests that he possesses the repertoire of ideological convictions, let alone the self-conscious intent, to cloak himself in the dark mantle of fascism. *The Art of the Deal* is not *Mein Kampf.*

Facile comparisons between past and present may reveal less about the lineage of the new authoritarianism than about our own need to express our condemnation in the strongest possible terms. "Fascism," after all, is a term of polemical exigency that makes itself available in political discourse whenever the more subtle work of political analysis seems to fail. In rhetoric there is a name for this habit of invoking fascism: it is called "Godwin's law." Needless to say, we should not rest easy, confident that Trumpism will not undergo an ideological transformation into actual fascism. But such a shift seems unlikely. Whatever Trumpism may be, it is not the fascism of a personality type, or a fascism that would necessarily enact what it threatens. It is the political consequence of a mediatized public sphere in which politics in the substantive sense is giving way to the commodification of politics, and politicians themselves are scrutinized less for their policies than for their so-called brands. It would be hard to deny, of course, that many items from the original list of features describing the authoritarian personality map easily onto Trumpism, especially its chauvinism and swagger and its "tough-minded" style. (Curiously, sexual repression would seem to be a point of discontinuity: Trump has traded the older American convention of sexual moralism for sexual boasting, a change that has not inhibited his appeal among American evangelicals.) But such a list may remind us that the original fascist movements of the last century were already on their way to becoming a politics of mere *form*. If the comparison to fascism remains valid today, it may have less to do with specific points of ideology than with the replacement of ideology by a simplified language of self-promotion, which now characterizes all politics in an era of mass communication. To the authors of *Dialectic of Enlightenment*, the comparison between fascism and advertising was already self-evident: "The blind and rapidly spreading repetition of designated words links advertising to the totalitarian slogan.

The layer of experience which made words human like those who spoke them has been stripped away, and in its prompt appropriation language takes on the coldness which hitherto was peculiar to billboards and the advertising sections of newspapers."[54]

The Frankfurt School already grasped the crucial point: that fascism does not signify a radical break from mass democracy but only emerges as an intensification of its inner pathologies. More specifically, it recognized that capitalist systems of production and consumption do not leave intact the "real" interests of democratic citizens, however much they may still imagine that elections and other mechanisms of representative democracy permit them to express their "real" preferences. We simply cannot speak about the expression of genuine preferences in liberal democratic systems when a profusion of sociocultural norms shapes these preferences in advance. If this was the case when nativist movements reared their heads in the United States in the 1940s, it is all the more true today, when the logic of neoliberalism has extended its reach into all domains of life. As an illustration, it may suffice to quote from Max Horkheimer's introduction to *Prophets of Deceit: A Study in the Techniques of the American Agitator*, an undeservedly neglected 1949 work by Leo Löwenthal and Norbert Guterman. "Today," Horkheimer writes, "under the conditions of a highly industrialized society, consumption is largely determined by production even in the field of ideologies. Attitudes and reactive behavior are often 'manufactured.' The people do not 'choose' them freely but accept them under the pressure of power, real or imaginary."[55]

I have tried here to bring out the importance of this insight with special reference to Adorno's skeptical remarks on social psychology. According to Adorno, it would be mistaken to explain fascism by appealing to psychological categories, not least because psychologism carries a serious risk of depoliticization. Ironically enough, this depoliticizing gesture may appear altogether natural to those of us who feel that our methods of research must somehow reflect our "democratic" commitments.

Our democratic understanding of the self encourages us to interpret any political stance as the self-chosen expression of an authentic desire. But it is this "democratic" interpretation of political ideology as an autonomous expression that Horkheimer challenges in the passage just quoted. Even if sociopolitical pathologies are derived from real psychological pathologies, dialectical analysis cannot stop with this derivation but must seek the prior social conditioning that first constitutes the psyche as something real.[56] In his unpublished "Remarks," Adorno presses this point even further. Under the conditions of late-modern capitalism, the cultural and social forces that shape even the innermost features of personal need and desire have grown so overwhelming that the very categories of need and desire are called into question.

All of the above, of course, may invite skepticism. In recent decades, the Frankfurt School's analysis of the culture industry has admittedly lost much of its luster, in part because its extreme fatalism harmonizes so poorly with democratic sensibilities. But refuting a line of social criticism simply because it is felt to be an affront to one's political aspirations is a questionable (if commonplace) practice. Adorno, we should recall, anticipated precisely this kind of resistance in his remarks on "democratic bias" in social research. But he could hardly have anticipated the strange phenomenon whereby his own name would circulate as a commodity (in the form, for example, of Eric Jarosinski's satirical book *Nein*, which sports an image of Adorno on the cover and might one day sell far more copies than any book by Adorno himself). It was Adorno's greatest misfortune that some of his most memorable aphorisms would survive him only to become a series of quotable clichés. In an ironic turn he might have appreciated, the culture industry today has taken its final vengeance by penetrating the very realm of criticism, transforming intellectuals themselves into paragons of late-capitalist celebrity.[57] "In psychoanalysis," Adorno observed, "nothing is true except the exaggerations."[58] This *aperçu* is itself an exaggeration, and it ranks among the most readily abused phrases in the Adornian archive. But today it may call for revision. After all, psychoanalytic categories remain valid only so long as we can plausibly speak of the psyche as a real referent. What passes for politics today in the United States has its etiology not in determinate forms of psychological character but rather in modes of mindless spectacle that may awaken doubt as to whether the "mind" remains a useful category of political analysis.

But precisely this claim (which I have admittedly stated with some exaggeration) may permit us to retain at least a core insight from the research program discussed at the start of this chapter. It was a guiding premise of the Frankfurt School that one might develop, through psychoanalysis, a correlation between individual psychology and ideological commitment. But Adorno wished to inject into the *AP* research agenda a more radical insight, which later efforts to revise the idea of the authoritarian personality may have neglected, namely, that psychological character itself is conditional upon historically variant social and culture forms. Rather than tracing the lineage of an occurrence of authoritarian consciousness, we might, following Adorno's cue, trace that authoritarianism to a standardization of consciousness that today leaves no precinct of our culture unmarked.

This problem has reemerged in the recent scandal about "data-harvesting" by Cambridge Analytica, a private data-analysis firm that advertises its services for both commercial and political uses. By the summer of 2014 the firm was promising to create "psychometric profiles" of American voters, who could then be targeted with ideological content calibrated with apparent precision according to their personality types. The public scandal surrounding Cambridge Analytica (which received lavish funding from the Republican donor Robert Mercer and offered its services to the Trump presidential campaign) has mostly focused on the question of whether data from more than fifty million Facebook users was gained by illegal means or without informed consent.[59] But the deeper question is how the firm could plausibly claim that its psychometric profiles and correlated voter categories would be accurate at all. Anyone who logs into social media will see how its users indulge in the strange ritual of categorizing themselves by answering questionnaires, and then happily announcing the results to all of those whom the system has encouraged them to define as their "friends." Such questionnaires often pose questions in the innocent categories of mass culture ("Which Harry Potter Character Are You?") that must strike even the participants as a harmlessly ironic game of postmodern totemism.

But people rarely pause to ask themselves just what the responses are supposed to reveal, and in what ways the preformed categories of the commercial domain could plausibly be said to correlate with preexisting psychological and political tendencies. One possibility is that they do not, or that they reveal much less about voter (or buyer) preference than companies such as Cambridge Analytica want their high-paying clients to believe. The worry here is not only that these psychometric tests impose rigid typolologies on a fluid and diverse human reality; the deeper problem is that they grant their own typologies the illusory determinism of natural kinds. But is this *entirely* mistaken? It is worth pondering the striking similarity between the modern typologies of social psychology, with their data-rich prestige and appearance of objective science, and the older typologies of astrology ("Which zodiac sign are you?"), which once enjoyed a similar illusion of objectivity and condemned each individual to the determinism of the stars. Trust in the objective power of constellations over human life appears as an instance of what Adorno, in his study of the *Los Angeles Times* astrology column, called "pseudo-rationality."[60] Whether "psychometric" data repeats the same occultism dressed up as pseudoscience remains an open question. This comparison, however, ignores a crucial difference, namely, that today's social media are an effective instrument for the *creation* of psychological and political types. The distinctions of the zodiac obviously have no bearing on who we are. But the way we carve up social reality helps to call such types into being to the degree that they become socially consequential or "real." The philosopher Ian Hacking has described this as the "looping effect of human kinds."[61] By opting voluntarily into the apparently "democratic" realm of massified culture, participants in the capitalist marketplace begin to resemble just those "effects" of the consumer types that the culture had imagined them to be. There is, we might conclude, a surprising continuity between the attempt in *The Authoritiarian Personality* to predict a susceptibility to fascism and the new "data-harvesting" techniques, which claim once again to identify this susceptibility, not to combat it but to exploit it for both commercial and political purposes. The true scandal of Cambridge Analytica may be that psychometric profiles are gaining an increased reality in both psychological and political life only because, as Adorno warned, human experience itself is growing increasingly standardized or "typed." In this degraded situation, it should hardly surprise us that only the most banal and regressive forms of political expression would emerge victorious.

The above considerations might alert us to the far more unsettling and ironic proposition that today *both* realms—the political and the psychological—are threatened with dissolution. Seen from this perspective, the attempt to describe Trumpism with the pathologizing language of character types works only as a defense against the deeper possibility that Trump, far from being a violation of the norm, actually signifies an emergent norm of the social order as such. If any of the foregoing is correct, then we should countenance the sobering proposition that, even if Trump himself had suffered an electoral defeat, the social phenomena that made him possible can be expected to grow only more powerful in the future.

NOTES

This essay was originally written as the opening lecture in the daylong series "Criticism and Theory in an Age of Populism," convened April 29, 2016, at Harvard University, on the occasion of the fortieth anniversary of the School of Criticism and Theory. My sincere thanks to Homi Babha and Hent de Vries for the invitation to present these remarks, and to the assembled audience for their comments. For the written version, I received exceptionally helpful comments from Judith Surkis, Martin Jay, Thomas Wheatland, Espen Hammer, Lawrence Glickman, and Jason Stanley. The essay was revised and published online at https://www.boundary2.org /2016/06/peter-gordon-the-authoritarian-personality-revisited -reading-adorno-in-the-age-of-trump/. It then appeared in the print edition of the journal *boundary2* 44, no. 2 (2017): 31–56. The version published here is substantially revised and expanded, and is reprinted with the kind permission of *boundary2*. My thanks to Charles Clavey for assistance with copyediting and especially for working on the footnotes and reformatting. I am also grateful for suggestions from the two anonymous readers of the manuscript submitted to the University of Chicago Press. Needless to say, all shortcomings in the current text are wholly my own responsibility.

1. Matthew MacWilliams, "The One Weird Trait That Predicts Whether You're a Trump Supporter," *Politico*, January 17, 2016, https://www.politico.com/magazine/story/2016/01/donald-trump -2016-authoritarian-213533.

2. More recently he has published his findings in a short book. See Matthew MacWilliams, *The Rise of Trump: America's Authoritarian Spring*, Public Works (Amherst, MA: Amherst College Press, 2016).

3. MacWilliams, "One Weird Trait."

4. Theodor W. Adorno et al., *The Authoritarian Personality* (New York: Harper & Brothers, 1950). All citations are to this original (unabridged) version.

5. Theodor W. Adorno and Max Horkheimer, *Dialectic of Enlightenment: Philosophical Fragments*, ed. Gunzelin Noerr, trans. Edmund Jephcott (Stanford, CA: Stanford University Press, 2002), 94–136.

6. Stefan Müller-Doohm, *Adorno: A Biography*, trans. Rodney Livingstone (Malden, MA: Polity Press, 2009), 292.

7. Adorno et al., *Authoritarian Personality*, 1.

8. Adorno et al., *Authoritarian Personality*, 228.

9. Adorno et al., *Authoritarian Personality*, 228.

10. Adorno et al., *Authoritarian Personality*, 194.

11. Adorno et al., *Authoritarian Personality*, 222.

12. Adorno et al., *Authoritarian Personality*, 228.

13. Erich Fromm, *The Working Class in Weimar Germany: A Psychological and Sociological Study*, ed. Wolfgang Bonss, trans. Barbara Weinberger (Leamington Spa, Warwickshire, UK: Berg Publishers, 1984).

14. Wilhelm Reich, *The Mass Psychology of Fascism*, trans. Vincent R. Carfagno (New York: Farrar Straus Giroux, 1970); Max Horkheimer, Erich Fromm, and Herbert Marcuse, *Studien über Autorität und Familie* (Studies on Authority and the Family), vol. 5 (Paris: F. Alcan, 1936).

15. Martin Jay, *The Dialectical Imagination: A History of the Frankfurt School and the Institute of Social Research, 1923–1950* (Boston: Little, Brown, 1973), 113–42, 219–52.

16. Adorno et al., *Authoritarian Personality*, ix.

17. Adorno et al., *Authoritarian Personality*, vii.

18. Adorno et al., *Authoritarian Personality*, vii.

19. Thomas Wheatland, *The Frankfurt School in Exile* (Minneapolis: University of Minnesota Press, 2009), 257.

20. Jos Meloen, "The Fortieth Anniversary of 'The Authoritarian Personality,'" *Politics and the Individual* 1, no. 1 (1991): 119–27.

21. Jay, *Dialectical Imagination*, 248–50.

22. John Levi Martin, "'The Authoritarian Personality,' 50 Years Later: What Lessons Are There for Political Psychology?," *Political Psychology* 22, no. 1 (2001): 1.

23. Nevitt Sanford, "A Personal Account of the Study of Authoritarianism: Comment on Samuelson," *Journal of Social Issues* 42, no. 1 (1986): 209–14; quoting Adorno et al., *Authoritarian Personality*, 975.

24. Crucial insight into the early and promising phase of conversation between the émigré intellectuals and American social scientists can be found in Wheatland, *Frankfurt School in Exile*, and Thomas Wheatland, "Franz L. Neumann: Negotiating Political Exile," in *German Historical Institute Bulletin*, supplement 10, ed. Jan Logemann and Mary Nolan (New York: Cambridge University Press, 2014), 111–38.

25. Müller-Doohm, *Adorno*, 296.

26. Adorno et al., *Authoritarian Personality*, 749; my emphasis.

27. Adorno et al., *Authoritarian Personality*, 747; my emphasis.

28. Wheatland, *The Frankfurt School in Exile*, 244; my emphasis. Wheatland concludes that "it would appear that Horkheimer and Adorno may never have fully bought into the premises and methodology underlying *The Authoritarian Personality*. If I am correct, Adorno's utterances that undercut the project are probably closer to his actual position on the topic, and his contributions to the book are an accommodation to American research, as well as to the pragmatic aims of the AJC and American social scientific collaborators." Thomas Wheatland, private correspondence, May 31, 2016.

29. Theodor W. Adorno, "Remarks on *The Authoritarian Personality*" (unpublished, 1948), 1–2, Max Horkheimer Archive Universitätsbibliothek, Goethe Universität, Frankfurt am Main, sammlungen.ub.uni-frankfurt.de/horkheimer/content/zoom /6323018?zoom=1&lat=1600&lon=1000&layers=B.

30. Adorno, "Remarks," 2.

31. Adorno, "Remarks," 11.

32. Adorno, "Remarks," 2.

33. Adorno, "Remarks," 2.

34. Adorno, "Remarks," 5.

35. Adorno, "Remarks," 29.

36. Adorno, "Remarks," 29.

37. Adorno, "Remarks," 28.

38. Adorno, "Remarks," 13.

39. Jay quotes Löwenthal in one of his epigraphs to chap. 6, "Aesthetic Theory and the Critique of Mass Culture." Jay, *Dialecti-*

cal Imagination, 173. Others have incorrectly attributed the saying to Adorno, as Jay notes in "Introduction to a Festschrift for Leo Löwenthal on His Eightieth Birthday," in *Permanent Exiles: Essays on the Intellectual Migration from Germany to America* (New York: Columbia University Press, 1986), 101.

40. Theodor W. Adorno, "Freudian Theory and the Pattern of Fascist Propaganda (1951)," in *Essential Frankfurt School Reader*, ed. Andrew Arato and Eike Gephardt (New York: Continuum Books, 1987), 135.

41. Adorno, "Freudian Theory," 134.

42. Adorno, "Freudian Theory," 134; my emphasis.

43. Adorno, "Freudian Theory," 135.

44. Adorno, "Freudian Theory," 135; my emphasis.

45. Adorno, "Freudian Theory," 136–37.

46. Adorno, "Freudian Theory," 125.

47. Adorno, "Freudian Theory," 127.

48. Adorno, "Freudian Theory," 127.

49. Adorno, "Freudian Theory," 135; Peter E. Gordon, *Adorno and Existence* (Cambridge, MA: Harvard University Press, 2016).

50. Adorno, "Remarks," 11.

51. Michael Rogin, *Ronald Reagan, the Movie and Other Episodes in Political Demonology* (Berkeley: University of California Press, 1988).

52. Dennis W. Johnson and Brian C. Tringali, eds., "Message-Testing in the Twenty-First Century," in *Routledge Handbook of Political Management*, Routledge International Handbooks (New York: Routledge, 2010), 113–25.

53. Tim Carman, "Trump Steaks Are So Rare, We Can't Even Find One," *Washington Post*, March 23, 2016, https://www.washingtonpost.com/lifestyle/food/hey-trump-wheres-the-beef-trump-steaks-are-so-rare-we-cant-even-find-one/2016/03/22/175b682a-ebc3-11e5-bc08-3e03a5b41910_story.html.

54. Adorno and Horkheimer, *Dialectic of Enlightenment: Philosophical Fragments*, 135.

55. Max Horkheimer, introduction to Leo Löwenthal and

Norbert Guterman, *Prophets of Deceit: A Study in the Techniques of the American Agitator* (New York: Harper & Brothers, 1949), xi.

56. This refusal to rest content with the individual mind as the ontologically prior ground of political events is a theme shared by a wide range of social theorists, including Adorno and Foucault.

57. For a related diagnosis of this phenomenon, one might consider John Gray's remarks about Slavoj Žižek: "The role of global public intellectual Žižek performs has emerged along with a media apparatus and a culture of celebrity that are integral to the current model of capitalist expansion." Gray, "The Violent Visions of Slavoj Žižek," *New York Review of Books*, July 12, 2012, http://www.nybooks.com/articles/2012/07/12/violent-visions-slavoj-zizek/.

58. Theodor W. Adorno, *Minima Moralia: Reflections on a Damaged Life*, trans. E. F. N. Jephcott (New York: Verso, 2005), 49.

59. See the early revelation of the scandal he *New York Times*, https://www.nytimes.com/2018/03/17/us/politics/cambridge-analytica-trump-campaign.html (accessed March 30, 2018).

60. Theodor W. Adorno, *The Stars Come Down to Earth, and Other Essays on the Irrational in Culture*, ed. Stephen Crook (New York: Routledge, 1994).

61. Ian Hacking, "The Looping Effects of Human Kinds," in *Causal Cognition: A Multidisciplinary Debate*, ed. Dan Sperber, David Premack, and Ann James Premack (Oxford: Oxford Universty Press, 1996).

RADICAL CRITIQUE AND LATE EPISTEMOLOGY

TOCQUEVILLE, ADORNO, AND
AUTHORITARIANISM

Max Pensky

Bad political times compel political theorists to reassess their cherished concepts, methods, and assumptions, and rightly so. The current of revitalized authoritarianism, xenophobia, and hostility to democratic political culture that has afflicted so many countries over the past decade surely counts as bad political times, and there is no end in sight. For political theorists grappling with making these authoritarian trends comprehensible—and contributing to the effort to reverse or at least slow them—the task of revisiting and, if necessary, transforming our practice is both a professional and a political responsibility. For many political scientists, an emerging age of peril for democratic governance worldwide comes as a shock for which neither they nor their standard assumptions were prepared. Terms like democratic backsliding, retrogression, deconsolidation, and disconnection express more than a social-scientific interest in the variability of performance of democratic systems, or the project of assessing the risk of authoritarian political transitions.[1] They evoke a panicked sense of things coming apart, of solid things melting into air.

Understanding the root causes of such systemic pathologies in democracies would require a broad spectrum of different approaches. At the institutional level, a theory of democratic decline would need to explain how political institutions that had been considered durable, from parliamentary procedure to constitutional essentials and the rule of law, have now come under such enormous pressure that they are less and less able to withstand authoritarian, xenophobic, and populist pressures. Just as important, at the micro level of subjective attitudes, values, and commitments, a theory of democratic deconsolidation and authoritarian risks would have to address where these pressures come from and what is happening to the hearts and minds of democratic citizens to make deconsolidation appear not only possible but desirable to so many of them. Standard social-scientific theories of democratic deconsolidation usually attempt to answer these latter questions via qualitative methods, eliciting responses to questions designed to make transformations in subjective attitudes and motivations observable and measurable. These methods assume "deep," "latent," or "underlying" authoritarian attitudes, values, or affects, lying submerged in the hidden strata of the psychic and motivational life of democratic citizens, attitudes that can be "triggered" or "activated" (according to the metaphor of the dog whistle) by changing conditions and motivated political leaders.[2] These authoritarian psychic contents can, with difficulty, be elicited by the social scientist, and once properly collated form a data set that can be analyzed for significant correlations between measurable attitudinal changes and other transformations of the political system. In this way one can develop suggestive hypotheses regarding the decline of democratic civil society, voter disaffection, growing levels of rage, resentment and discontent, or the spread of antidemocratic sentiments.

This is has been the core ambition of theories of authoritarianism, and of democratic fragility, at least since *The Authoritarian Personality*. But such theories share a weakness: they postulate, but cannot really establish, that the model of authoritarianism—deep or latent, hidden prejudices that are activated or triggered by external, antidemocratic forces—is a coherent or accurate one. Their standard qualitative methods implicitly draw on lightly defended assertions regarding rationality, agency, cogency, and other standard epistemic demands, postulating an interior of largely prepolitical subjectivity that can be identified and assessed by its externalization as responses to the scientists' polls, questionnaires, or focus groups. But what if these assumptions themselves are brought into question? What if authoritarianism as democracy's other is not the surface expression, via social-scientific method, of otherwise deep and occluded, reviled and tabooed personality contents? What if the nature of liberal democratic life itself produces new forms of political subjectivity in which this very model of surface and depth no longer applies? If authoritarianism is not the mythic return of democracy's long-buried other, but part of the physiognomy of liberal democracy itself? What social-scientific method would register *that* possibility?

Critical theorists, whose relation with the broader field of political theory is fraught enough, obviously have a relative advantage over many of their peers in this, though it's not an unproblematic one. If it means anything, the tradition of Frankfurt School critical theory offers a radical social critique indicting the very idea that democratic life or democratic subjectivity exhibit an identifiable and stable form of socially embodied reason, while authoritarianism is liberal democracy's dark and latent other. Under conditions of neoliberal capitalism, the assumptions regarding the relative stability and cogency of the individual rational agent are themselves the objects rather than the initiating conditions of radical critique. Democracy and its other—the slide into authoritarian rule and the disappearance of the rational agency of individual political actors—are not two stark possibilities but twin, mutually generating modalities of the same human condition. In *Dialectic of Enlightenment*, Adorno and Horkheimer had asserted that this condition can be traced back to the emergence of human sapience and forward to the smallest details of contemporary life under the culture industry, including micro-level pathologies of comportment, sensibility, gesture, habit, and psychology.

The bleakness of this global critique, and the implicit claim that no coherent political practical response is possible in the face of a homogenous and omnipresent form of social domination, have frequently evoked charges of quietism and elitism, even incoherence or self-contradiction. For a radical and globalizing critique indicting liberal democracy for generating the conditions it associates with its authoritarian other must exempt itself from its own critique: in one way or another, no matter what methodological postulates a radical critique endorses, it must keep open the possibility that the *totaler Verblendungszusammenhang*, the total context of delusion, is not total.

This is a standard feature in the traditional reception history of the Frankfurt School. For all its familiarity, this feature remains just as cogent and pressing now as it was when Lukács dismissed Adorno's work as emanating from the "Grand Hotel Abyss."[3] If we ourselves are to respond with critical insight and cogency to the political bad times that are upon us, we need to take this debate as unfinished.

The claim that democratic decline and the advent of authoritarian attitudes occur primarily through the internal transformation of the epistemic and motivational capacities of (formerly) democratic citizens is certainly not unique to the Frankfurt School theorists, or to Adorno in particular. A critical theory of democratic deconsolidation is only one variant of a far older family of declensionist narratives, in which a once robust democratic civil society succumbs to its own internal pathologies. What is distinct about the version of democratic decline that Adorno offered in the 1940s and 1950s, however, is the richness with which Adorno takes up some of the more vexing problems of methodology that so many other variants of this family of critical theories either gloss over or fail to register entirely.

Peter Gordon's analysis (in this volume) vividly reconstructs Adorno's awareness of the limitations and paradoxes arising from the attempt to use empirical methods to explain the transformation of political subjectivity, even as he participated in some of the most influential early qualitative assessment of democratic decline in *The Authoritarian Personality*. Adorno, it seems, had a growing suspicion that such methods were inherently inadequate to their task.

What else did Adorno offer as a response to these limitations? Adorno's work in the period roughly between the publication of *Minima Moralia*, in 1951, and *Negative Dialectics*, fifteen years later, exhibits a near-constant effort to account for the possibility of a radical social critique beyond the limitations of empirical methodology. It was a search for a way of registering and describing the gradual decay of subjects' capacities for political experience and political agency, as the mechanics of social domination extend steadily into previously uncolonized areas of subjectivity. It also posed the question of whether "the individual"—the deeply ambivalent historical achievement of bourgeois modernity—was likely to survive the advent of mass culture and newer, more effective forms of social domination.

What I will argue in this chapter is that Adorno's postwar efforts to develop an alternative method for a radical critique of the subjective dimensions of authoritarianism paralleled, to a striking degree, a far earlier attempt to do very much the same thing, though at the *beginning*, rather than the *end*, of the era of liberal democratic political culture. I will contrast Adorno's project with that of Alexis de Tocqueville, in *Democracy in America*: his prediction of the collapse of just that subject, of democratic deconsolidation ("democratic despotism," as Tocqueville would reluctantly label it) and the advent of a kind of proto-authoritarianism, in the middle of the nineteenth century.

At either end of the period of bourgeois liberal democracy, Tocqueville and Adorno developed closely observed phenomenologies of the small details of democratic decline. They did so by attending to the visible surface effects of democratic life: not by deducing deep structures but by describing visible affects, bodily gestures and motions, comportment and carriage, elements of the somatic makeup of subjects that could illuminate in a pointillist manner a larger, systemic or macro-level pathology. It's in this shared approach that we can find productive and challenging continuities between Adorno's work, most notably in *Minima Moralia* from 1951, and Tocqueville's *Democracy in America* from 1835 (volume 1) and 1840 (volume 2).

For our purposes, what links Tocqueville and Adorno most closely is not, or at least not principally, their American sojourns, significant as those trips surely were.[4] While America remained a vital model for democratic culture for both, their predictions for the decline of that culture were not limited to the special case of American political life. They described a postnational, systemic pathology that applied as much, and in some respects more, to European democratization, which entailed the loss of an aristocratic, openly inegalitarian culture.

Tocqueville's writing in the 1830s, and Adorno's in the 1940s, both describe a vicious circle operating between subjectivity and the institutions of public political life—between unit and structure—leading to the dysfunction and fading of the latter and the pathological distortion of the former. Both propose that macro-level institutional dysfunction can be predicted and diagnosed through changes in the observable *habitus* of subjects occupying those institutions. Both propose that such subjective changes are accessible through a kind of close phenomenology of the way in which subjective affects and attitudes register through small material details of social existence.

This *micrological* phenomenological approach—requiring close observation and description of a range of phenomena that otherwise appear unrelated; judicious attention to the small, telling detail; and sensitivity to particulars—is distinct from familiar qualitative social-scientific methods, which of course Tocqueville had no access to, and Adorno had come, rightly, to mistrust.

Underlying the capacity for attention that both Tocqueville

and Adorno bring to their American observations, and translate into their radical critiques of the fate of political subjectivity in liberal democracies, is an epistemic stance characterized by a high degree of self-reflexivity. Both men *know* that describing the phenomena of democratic decline demands epistemic tools and approaches that are, in one way or another, alien to the new world they confront. This alienness is utterly distinct from the familiar appeal to the detachment of the intellectual, or the neutral observer perspective of the empirical social scientist. As a self-reflexive cognitive stance, it is a deliberate, critical refunctioning of epistemic aptitudes and talents that are in the process of vanishing from the democratizing world, through the very social and political processes that are their subject matter.

Both Tocqueville and Adorno, in other words, consciously draw on their own peculiar status as epistemically antiquated—as *late*—as a way of gaining access to features of a postsubjective political landscape that otherwise remain occluded. In both cases, this self-awareness of lateness entails a complex relation to their own status as elites, and the fading of the world that made that status possible.

Tocqueville and Adorno both deploy versions of late epistemology: in Tocqueville's case, this lateness can be reconstructed through his close descriptions of American life, and their implications for a postdemocratic future. In Adorno's case, of course, an entire philosophical vision, negative dialectics, lies behind the notion of epistemic lateness as I mean it, an approach that cannot even be adequately summarized here. In brief, however, both Tocqueville and Adorno see themselves as observers interpreting a field of phenomena by using concepts and capacities that were developed in, and remain tied to, a cultural, historical, and political reality whose own passing is part of the very phenomena in question. Their characteristic modes of thought are implicated in the process they wish to describe, in the sense of a growing obsolescence and aging.

In Tocqueville's case, this late epistemology rests on a

conscious appropriation of the finesse of distinctions and attention to particularities, aptitudes he sees as a remnant of a vanishing aristocratic world. For Adorno, the micrological description
of the waning of the institution of (bourgeois) subjectivity, and
its replacement with a mode of administered consciousness, depends in large measure on his self-reflection on the loss of self,
the experience of the decay of the capacity to experience, in the
transition from a high-bourgeois political culture of the European nineteenth century to the mass culture of the American
twentieth.

Tocqueville's visit to the United States was the provocation
for an attempt to understand the systemic pathologies of democratic life that would, in one way or another, express themselves
in the motivations and habits, the *moeurs* and everyday normative orientations, of democratic subjects. While Adorno, of
course, spent over a decade in the United States as an exile and
refugee struggling for (and just as often against) some form of
social integration, Tocqueville's brief and largely enjoyable tour
of the eastern United States, ostensibly to research a study of
the American penal system, seems hardly adequate to ground a
large-scale theory of democratic decline. And yet the men were
alike in their peculiar capacity for attention, even if it was often,
perhaps by necessity, supplemented by a considerable ability to
miss forests for trees. As is frequently noted, Adorno's American
years were not exactly a period of immersive cultural attention.
For the most part, the American mass culture he observed was
limited to the hardly typical examples of the Upper West Side and
Pacific Palisades, along with gingerly consumption of American
mass media.[5] By contrast Tocqueville was a notorious cultural
sponge, who in his six months arguably traveled far more widely,
and deeply, than Adorno in his thirteen years.

On another level, however, the respective theories of democratic decline that these American journeys made possible were
not ultimately, or perhaps even primarily, about American democracy. The alienation of geographical and cultural distance—

the extreme strangeness of American political and cultural life—made possible a series of reflections that both men understood as referring directly to the European context, in relation to which both stood partly on the outside. As Claus Offe has aptly noted, it would be a costly misunderstanding to see the American experience as offering any simple geographical or temporal contrast to the old Europe, whose democratization Tocqueville saw as impending and inevitable and Adorno saw as senescent and vanishing.[6] Compared to Europe, the United States was for them neither merely distant nor merely new, neither utterly strange nor uncannily familiar. What both men drew from their American visits was a kind of temporal disturbance—a convolution or complication of time, narrative, and narratability, of meaning and its enabling conditions—too subtle for the standard idea of "old" Europe confronting "new" American democracy.

*
**

The second volume of Tocqueville's *Democracy in America* famously concludes with the prediction of "democratic despotism," a crystallization of formerly vibrant democratic culture marking the end of the heroic era of bourgeois democracy by squeezing off the sources of political agency among equally constituted citizens. The quintessence of political experience for Tocqueville is the capacity for the exercise of political freedom in concert—an expanded self only possible in the democratic political space. And yet that same republican space, dependent on formal-legal equality, will for Tocqueville inevitably close as the expanded agency narrows to accommodate the individualism—Tocqueville's shorthand for the pathology of democratic decline—generated as subjects wrestle with the material consequences of formal equality.

Tocqueville had commented earlier in *Democracy in America* about the (for him) remarkable "Cartesianism" of American democratic culture. By this he meant that a democratic political culture that had freed itself from all traditional hierarchies of inherited rank and social distinction, of predetermined value, must organize itself through the fundamental rational principle of Descartes's philosophical modernism, and accordingly take the work of valuation of life and assignment of meaning as a rational exercise where method triumphs over outcome. Once all traditional sources of meaning have melted into air, tradition as such can be received only as so much information, its value assigned according to subjective imperatives. All social formations are equally liable to rational evaluation by the individual according to ultimately arbitrary standards; all habits, values, and norms are in principle intelligible only as material for individual judgment and calculation.

This formal equality of rational evaluation is a triumph of democratic equality. But according to the familiar story of the dynamics of social modernization (which both Nietzsche and Weber would, in a half century, come to concentrate on), persons are thrown onto their own resources for identifying the best way to make valuations of the rules, habits, and forms of living to which they assign value.[7] Those resources prove too meager and fragile to sustain the work of producing and maintaining a political existence.

This shortcoming includes the reproduction of the value of collective political agency in relation to that of individual satisfaction, material comfort, and security. Tocqueville suspects that for this specific version of American Cartesianism (which we would nowadays refer to as a facet of neoliberalism), the material incentives of comparative personal advantage, risk management, physical comfort, and expressive affluence will crowd out the psychic room required for the demanding project of collective self-governance, whose attractions and incentives are far more diffuse and deferred.

Formal legal and political equality engender a shift in the motivational bases of democratic subjects, imperceptibly eroding capacities for political agency as they realign the incentives for subjects to individuate. Democratic conditions of formal equality crystallize in a new imperative toward "individualism," a term that Tocqueville famously coins, and which he associates strongly with a trend toward voluntary self-isolation and withdrawal from associational life, a form of isolation and atomization that Arendt would later identify as the kernel of loneliness at the heart of totalitarianism.[8] Crucially, Tocqueville does not want to distinguish a political from an economic conception of individualism, implying that conditions of formal political equality, consistently imposed, generate from within themselves a dynamic for persons not only to individuate themselves but to understand this individuation as an open-ended process of increase in material well-being, one that is coupled with an interminable anxiety about the relative weight of well-being in comparison with that of equally situated others.

Individualism, Tocqueville thinks, rests on a sort of simple but evidently unavoidable epistemic error by members of a democratic, egalitarian political order. In contrast to the essentially predemocratic vice of selfishness, individualism is specific to modern democratic life and arises from "defects of the mind as much as vices of the heart" (482). As a general loss of political solidarity, individualism arises from the misjudgment that political life is at every point compatible with increasing material well-being and spiritual self-sufficiency. Once acted upon by a sufficient number of citizens, this misjudgment touches off a process of physical and social disaggregation, a cycle that is self-fueled insofar as the ebbing of solidary associational political life also becomes a cause and no longer a mere outcome of the tropism away from collective political action.

This transforms the attitudes and motivations that subjects bear toward democratic political authority most of all. As Patrick Deneen has pointed out, a core feature of Tocqueville's theory of democratic decline is the claim that the liberal demand for the strict equality of individually free actors generates contradictory expectations on the part of subjects: a simultaneous insistence that their individual autonomy suffer no injury, and a longing for an all-powerful state to attend to their resentments in response to perceived inequities.[9] Citizens undergo steady pressures to shift responsibility for governance toward tutelary powers that assume responsibility for a higher and higher share of risk management and for the provision of predictable conditions, while at the same time, somewhat perversely, maintaining their claims for political self-determination through periodic elections, events that drift from exercises of popular sovereignty to *ex post* diagnoses of existing macro-level dysfunction (an all too familiar feature of the current authoritarian turn). Depersonalizing the actual operation of sovereign power, citizens acquire dummy conceptions of individual autonomy, increasingly projecting fantasies of agency onto charismatic leaders even as the anonymization of political power slips ever further out of sight.

This introduces a serious risk for older-style, violence-based political despotism, of course. But despotism and anarchy, the two traditional outcomes of democratic failure, are for Tocqueville outweighed by a newer and stranger possibility, which he sees as without historical precedent. Consistently realized, a life of democratic equality results in the loss of the capacity for a specific form of political experience, of "the political life itself."[10]

This brings us to late epistemology. Tocqueville's insight into the psychic structure of democratic man and woman—his understanding of the "manners and morals" of life under equality—is, as many of his readers have shown, deeply linked to his own circumstance as a late member of a vanishing milieu of French aristocracy. In fact Tocqueville himself frequently regarded his ambivalent aristocratic legacy in epistemic terms. Where democratic equality tends to shepherd individual persons toward uniformity of thoughts, attitudes, incentives, and judgments, the epistemic repertoire adapted to an aristocratic political culture entails (for better and worse) the capacity to think in terms of distinctions, ambivalences, contrasts, differences, and particularities. Attentiveness to detail is a requisite for the capacity to read macro-level social formations from micro-level variations in speech, dress, or gesture. The capacity to diagnose the advent of a new Cartesianism, one could say, rests in the refunctioning of an old Montaignianism.

Democratic societies pressure persons to adopt "general ideas," Tocqueville thinks, a crucial term for which he characteristically gives multiple and not entirely compatible definitions, but which refers ultimately to a new and dominant cognitive practice, a sort of epistemic shortcut or hack, obviating the need for careful discernment and judgment through the use of labor-saving procedures in which otherwise distinct phenomena are clumped under titular headings, as "good enough" cognitive fits. General ideas derive from the practically necessary process of "enclosing a very great number of analogous objects under the same form so as to think about them more conveniently" (411). (Cognition as labor-saving is surely also an underappreciated aspect of the conception of *Zweckrationalität* from Weber through Horkheimer and Adorno.)

In this sense, general ideas are the precise counterpart of late epistemology, which, rooted in a fading predemocratic milieu, has become reflective and aesthetic, largely ornamental and too costly to practice—except perhaps here, in the capacity to register (with Tocqueville's characteristically ambivalent admixture of admiration and alarm) the potential of democracy to initiate a process of epistemic loss. Such general ideas mark sites in the individual democratic, "Cartesian" mind that might once have been capable of fuller forms of socially mediated experience. Replacing the costly work of deliberation, discrimination, and judgment, this emergent form of democratic cognition is tailored to the frenetic conditions of the quest for material abundance and legal equality. Carried out consistently, this emergent epistemology (or post-epistemology), linked internally to the new social institution of the individual, contributes to a transformed mentality, one that prefers to outsource the exercise of democratic power to a professionalized and remote tutelary authority, according to a tacit agreement to exchange liberty for comfort, peace, and wealth. It does just that—though for Tocqueville such a compact cannot and will not remain stable.

This kind of epistemic labor saving is, in large part, a way of coping with burdens of judgment more efficiently given the never-ending demands of a sort of global commercial imperative. The distinctive *busyness* of Americans—the unending bustle, the constant movement, the innumerable projects, causes, undertakings, and enterprises—struck Tocqueville as remarkable, and was a particular target of Tocqueville's ambivalence. Looked at as an emergent mode of subjective comportment, this American hustle struck Tocqueville as an admirable aspect of the advent of democratic self-governance. At the same time, he perceived that activity for its own sake, divorced from the expanded subjectivity of the collective work of politics, could just as easily be seen as a pathology, like the collective vibration of individual atoms leading to exhaustion. (The aged Kant may have sensed something closely related, in his worry that collective busyness, divorced from the invisible hand of providence to guide its progress toward a rational state, was mere "Abderitism," the anxious inability to keep still, pointlessly bustling idiocy.[11])

The labor-saving work of general ideas assists in the staccato, hair-trigger capacity to respond quickly to material incentives, which is good business. In part, too, the advent of general ideas is an outcome of gradually centralizing political administration and its own need for uniformity in its application of sovereign power.[12]

In this sense, Tocqueville's aristocratic late epistemology is in part the mere negation of democratic thinking, of inequality in terms of rank, hierarchy, or classificatory schemes. At the same time, he remained struck by the (for him) odd, distinctive *timelessness* of democratic thinking—the open hostility to temporality or chronicity in the use of concepts—which he contrasted to the aristocratic mind's preference for precedent, age, and tradition.[13] Tocqueville recognized these as modes of thinking that democratic life was sweeping away. He wasted little time mourning their loss, even as he contemplated the implications of their absence in the dramatic foreshortening of associational life. He knew his Burke and Le Maistre, and understood the conservative equation of democratic newness with old-style mob rule, finding it entirely unsatisfactory as an account of how democratic institutions could interact with "customs and habits" of citizens to generate stability rather than anarchy, just as he regarded conservatism as unsuited to identifying the newness of the kind of despotism that democratic societies were prone to.

Instead, Tocqueville saw his method, and his thinking, as the refunctioning of an epistemic *ancien régime*—as a capacity to hold particular objects and experiences *as* particular, to tarry in the rush to subsume particulars under general concepts; an alertness to subtle variations and gradual processes of change, especially of decline; a kind of hermeneutic sensitivity for the unintended expression of otherwise marginal expressions and communications; and a capacity for reflective judgment, in Kant's sense, that carried over from matters of taste to those of principle. Late epistemology has lost its social context and in this sense survived its own death. As Sheldon Wolin, perhaps Tocqueville's most incisive reader, puts it:

> The defeat of the old aristocratic world had deprived [Tocqueville] of his privileges but not of his history. Aristocracy had become disembodied, detached from political actualities, thus freeing it theoretically. Because he had been formally disinherited by the new world but actually advantaged by the old, a unique detachment was possible: too much the stranger to the new world to identify with it, too aware of the demise of the old to indulge in political necrolatry.... Aristocracy would now become a metaphor for loss, for the things passing out of the world, from manners to virtue, from taste to disinterestedness. It would come to bear witness to loss in a world so thoroughly numbed by relentless change as to be unable to discriminate between change of fashion and loss of meaning.[14]

It's not a "view from nowhere" but a view from somewhere gone, or going. It is out of joint with the new model of democratic mind. But for that reason, late epistemology can see what democracy cannot: what a democratic political culture will look like, once its individualizing dynamic has undermined the motivational sources for political participation. In terms of Tocqueville's account of "democratic despotism" this takes the form of the profound ambivalence of the kind of subjectivity he predicts.

Late epistemology in this sense is also the capacity to think diachronically in the face of a social imperative toward timelessness—that is, toward myth. In addition to a preserved sense of duration (the movement of generations, of "deep time" as a social reality rather than an epiphenomenon to be registered only in the calculation of interest and return on investment), aristocratic thinking here connotes something like the secular remnant of an older Christian practice that took temporality in general as an admonitory moral catechism about the danger of attaching too much value to transient human undertakings.[15] In the case of Tocqueville, democratic timelessness, the uncanny sense of an endless present of material consumption, can only be effectively named, and countered, by what Wolin describes as the "archaism" of critical thinking, which in relation to the eternal present has a shocking capacity reminiscent of Benjamin's dialectical image.[16]

Cast into the open field of formal-legal equality, the democratic individual longs for material wealth while simultaneously suspecting its lasting value. He regards social status as both all-important and bracketable at one and the same time. He calculates his economic chances with both irreducible anxiety and irrepressible, fact-resistant optimism. He both welcomes and is repulsed by the contingency and uncertainty of his economic fate, making him susceptible to deep resentment over structural economic disadvantages that he insists, all evidence to the contrary notwithstanding, on seeing in strictly interpersonal terms. This is what renders his optimism about his material prospects so brittle and volatile, so easy to flip into rage. He is passionately attached to a range of pleasures and satisfactions that he simultaneously recognizes as petty and degrading and, in the long run, as a form of drudgery. His anxiety in the face of difference increases in inverse proportion to his encounter of different people in his social world, rendering him unable to assess risk rationally, and leading him to project vague insecurities onto equally vague out-groups. His passion for equality is both insulted and buttressed by the prospect of deviance in others. He clings to his political rights with the passionate expectation that efficient political leadership will assume all of his public responsibilities.

This range of contradictory attitudes and impulses—the authoritarian personality, in short—is thus for Tocqueville less a buried substratum of antidemocratic psychic life that critique lays bare than a new form of individuality made only of surfaces. From the late epistemic vantage, it is the foreseeable outcome of the new mode of politics consistently pursued. It reflects an irresolvable polarity generated by formal democratic equality itself, structuring the democratic psyche more profoundly than anything else: on the one hand, an increasing preference for a purely negative liberty—to be let alone with one's things, not to be messed with—and on the other, a longing to be led, disburdened of the anxiety that accompanies negative freedom, enfolded in the protective arms of a tutelary power that will ensure "tranquility" and public order with minimal popular consultation. Domination in this sense seems likeliest to Tocqueville as a capillary and bureaucratic phenomenon, rather than an exercise of physical violence.[17]

It's easy to see how this conceptualization of mild, bureaucratic domination anticipates Adorno's later account of the capillary powers of the totally administered society, in which the culture industry operates in tandem with an anonymous administrative power, or for that matter Foucault's account of the rise of disciplinary practices and bio-power.

But to conclude merely by praising Tocqueville's own un-timeliness, his prescience, is to miss the point. What Tocqueville grasped in the early nineteenth century—and hence largely independently of the category of technology central to Adorno's later account—was that the processes that were transforming democratic society into something far more passive, slapdash, and unsteady were new, and needed to be distinguished sharply from all previous historical examples of political failure.[18] Explaining the historical novelty of mild or "democratic despotism," and its transformation of subjects into docile bodies, did not require any additional postulates (such as the explosive rise of new technologies or the culture industry) drawn from outside of the small set of political categories to which Tocqueville limits himself. This suggests that the radical critique that locates the sources of authoritarianism within the potentials of liberal democracy itself is not dependent on *additional* premises regarding the roles of mass culture or of technological innovation, even if the latter remain important supplements.

The phenomenon of modern individualism is therefore primary. Individualism, which Tocqueville understood as the foreseeable mental outcome of sustained existence under the rough equality of conditions, an ambivalent unity of contradictory longings, describes both a new mode of subjectivity and a new basis for political and bureaucratic control. Individualism for Tocqueville is the emblematic new mode for the production of political subjectivity, insofar as it gives the appearance of offering the materials for successful individuation while simultaneously imposing conformity and homogeneity on each and every subject.

In this sense, Tocqueville is careful to distinguish individualism from any personal attitude or disposition. It is a new social-epistemic dominant, a hegemon. Like Adorno, Tocqueville never suspects that individuals in this modern sense are anything other than effects of modern social and political institutions. We are, under conditions of democratic equality, *all* individuals; individualism is the phenomenon for the production of sameness through difference.

As Tocqueville defines it, individualism

> disposes each member of the community to sever himself from the mass of his fellows and to draw apart with his family and his friends, so that after he has thus formed a little circle of his own, he willingly leaves society at large to itself. . . . Selfishness blights the germ of all virtue; individualism, at first, only saps the virtue of public life, but in the long run it attacks and destroys all others and is at length absorbed in downright selfishness. Selfishness is a vice as old as the world, which does not belong to one form of society more than another; individualism is of democratic origin, and it threatens to develop in the same ratio as equality of conditions. (482)

As a social dominant, then, individualism is how one continues to be a subject, with all its ambivalences of emotion and motive, its incessant anxieties, exhausting energy, and incompatible wishes, once civil society has been drained of its significance and severed from the practice of political liberty, and political authority has shifted from the remarkable exercise in popular sovereignty Tocqueville saw in the township system in the United States to the form of a tutelary, anonymous state power. The political solidarity once generated through the intermediate institutions in civil society ebbs with them.[19] Tocqueville occasionally seems to have seen this dynamic as contingent and reversible, and at other times as virtually a natural process that can be slowed but not stopped. In either case, it points to a postpolitical condition in which the production and provision of wants and needs by the tutelary political power finally obliges persons to live in a postdemocracy that has no recognizable form of political association at all.

In this sense, the description of democratic despotism that Tocqueville offers at the end of *Democracy in America* should be understood not just as the imposition of a swollen state authority on a weakened civil society but as the situation in which civil society's relevance for politics ceases to exist, while subjects are no longer able even to notice that this vital connection has been severed. Centralization plus democratic equality equals individualism, which, in its own irresistible seismic motion, gradually progresses until the *formal* isolation of subjects results in the *real* dissociation of persons. Crucially, Tocqueville sees this scenario as one of oppression without an open oppressor, or a form of administrative despotism without a despot, a postpolitical outcome that he struggles to name.

In the early nineteenth century, Tocqueville is aware that "despotism" refers to a shopworn and too-comfortable taxonomy of forms of governance. He has good reason to be dissatisfied with the term he finally settles on. But no other term does justice to a world he senses is imminent but cannot yet make out with clarity.[20]

In an age obsessed with contracts of all kinds, no contract, real or implied, is now needed to sustain this mutual indifference of individuals in perpetuity, since a centralized state authority has absorbed not just resistance but the psychic foundations that might generate the motive for it:

> Above [individuals] an immense tutelary power is elevated, which alone takes charge of assuring their enjoyments and watching over their fate. It is absolute, detailed, regular, far-seeing, and mild. It would resemble paternal power if, like that, it had for its object to prepare men for manhood; but on the contrary, it seeks only to keep them fixed irrevocably in childhood; it likes citizens to enjoy themselves provided that they think only of enjoying themselves. It willingly works for their happiness; but it wants to be the unique agent and sole arbiter of that; it provides for their security, foresees and secures their needs, facilitates their pleasures, conducts their principal affairs, directs their industry, regulates their estates, divides their inheritances; can it not take away from them entirely the trouble of thinking and the pain of living? (663)

Omnipotent and (relatively) mild political domination, such that the dominated no longer recognize it as such, is compatible with (and may even require) the affective range of rage, resentment, fear, superstition, and paranoia among those it both constrains and produces. Tocqueville encourages us to consider that the mildness of modern domination can produce the unity of otherwise incompatible subjective affects: busyness and aimlessness, rage and complacency, fear and hope. The presumption of psychic depth, in which subjects are the repositories and agents of their own affective life, is precisely what Tocqueville's conception of individualism abandons. (In this too, Tocqueville is strikingly close to what Adorno would see as the capillary effects of instrumental rationality a century later.[21] Looking forward to Adorno's borrowing of Freudian categories, this affective range as characteristic of "individualism" corresponds to the uses Adorno made of "ego weakness" [*Ich-schwäche*] in *The Authoritarian Personality*.) As a character of the postdemocratic world, the "mature and calm" social formation of individualism is likewise compatible with, and may even require, the confused jumble of affects characterized by xenophobic populism (itself a group affect wholly dependent on general ideas) and what postdemocratic individuals tend to see when they look for modes of the practice of political liberty.

Tocqueville's trademark ambivalence here permits the otherwise contradictory claim that mildness and calmness as characteristics of political domination are compatible with the extremity of affect on the part of those dominated. The affects too, like subjective capacities and inclinations for judgment and discrimination, are in effect outsourced to an authority capable of remotely augmenting and diminishing the emotional lives of isolated individuals, who no longer register that they are not sources of spontaneity, in either their thinking or their feeling. The general effect of democratic despotism as enervation, as a sort of social stupor, a general dialing-down of the intensity of political life, may even require the production of affective extremities (resentment, rage, fear) as part of its operational protocol.[22]

Tocqueville stresses again and again this heterogeneity and strangeness, the advent of a new modality of power constituting rather than constraining or repressing subjects and bodies, as Foucault would later describe it. It is a power that creates rather than merely fulfills wants, erases rather than stifles rebellious imaginings of alternatives, dismantles rather than colonizes the "inner life" of its subjects via the social institution of the modern individual. The new mode of power is not merely effective psychically and institutionally. It is, crucially, global and surreptitious, covering the surface of society with

> a network of small, complicated, painstaking, uniform rules through which the most original minds and the most vigorous souls cannot clear a way to surpass the crowd; it does not break wills, but it softens them, bends them, and directs them; it rarely forces one to act, but it constantly opposes itself to one's acting; it does not destroy, it prevents things from being born; it does not tyrannize, it hinders, compromises, enervates, extinguishes, dazes, and finally reduces each nation to being nothing more than a herd of timid and industrious animals of which the government is the shepherd. (663)

This kind of florid denunciation of political modernity has long buttressed the Straussian view of Tocqueville as a paleoconservative critic of mass democracy in good standing.[23] The truth is more complicated. Faced with the task of describing an entirely new social reality in a language derived from shattered intellectual traditions, it's not surprising that Tocqueville, perhaps fumblingly but with enormous evocative power, conjures the image of men and women so pacified by state power that they offer up a kind of glassy-eyed approval to the very forces that an earlier mode of democratic life, whose traces survive in scattered and isolated pockets, would have identified as worthy of bourgeois revolution.

This is radical normative political theory, not travelogue or amateur ethnography. But it finds its normativity less in a conception of intact socially embodied reason than in an archaic epistemology offering resistance to the tropism toward uniformity, the indifference to difference, that is the distinctive feature of the democratic despotism it prophesies. That makes Tocqueville's epistemic lateness into a kind of elitism of the second order, for better and worse. It makes visible social processes that remain obscure to those undergoing them, exempting itself from these processes by a sustained performance of a form of thinking particulars through their social totality, aflame at the moment of its historical disappearance.

*
**

Stupidity is not a natural quality, but one socially produced and reinforced. THEODOR W. ADORNO, *MINIMA MORALIA*[24]

In the years following World War II, Theodor Adorno described, *in medias res*, the evaporation of the bases of democratic life that Tocqueville had forecast a century earlier. Like Tocqueville, Adorno struggled to find a methodology adequate for describing a phenomenon whose global reach and capillary effects threatened to overwhelm even the most dedicated of social critics. In part, these experiments drew from the disciplinary imperatives Adorno had inherited from philosophical interpretation and sociological research, whose limitations and ideological entanglements he attempted to make visible even as he appropriated them. As a *Schriftsteller*, he consciously developed a highly personalized and distinctive, notoriously difficult mode of reflection and expression, ill-suited perhaps either to speculative philosophy or to sociological research, but (when the match between his observational gifts and its objects was favorable) capable of enormous critical power.

One way to describe this writing is as a sustained performance of a sense of lateness or disappointment, encompassing both epistemic and affective modes. Like Tocqueville, Adorno uses his own epistemic lateness—in this case, dialectical thinking, the mode befitting his status as the world's last bourgeois—as a lens through which otherwise unnoted moments in the rise of social domination come into focus.

This section of the chapter offers a reading of passages of Adorno's *Minima Moralia* as a counterpart to the second volume of Tocqueville's *Democracy in America*. Both books are chronicles of the experiences of a late European theorist in democratic America, but they share a deeper aim as well. They are attempts to mobilize late epistemology to describe democratic deconsolidation and its incremental replacement by a postdemocratic, authoritarian *habitus*—the waning of the form of subjectivity requisite for associational political life—a process that, by its nature as "mild" or capillary, is no longer epistemically accessible to those on whom it acts.

For Adorno, the progressive realization of a "totally administered society" describes the triumph of instrumental reason, penetrating into each and every social practice, liquidating from within the historical institution of bourgeois subjectivity. In a way highly complementary to Tocqueville, such a social power forecloses the space of subjective and collective political autonomy by inserting administrative and economic imperatives into the psychic structures of the erstwhile subjective agent. Instrumental imperatives capture and repurpose the individual, the very object of Tocqueville's alarm, erecting in its place a sort of taxidermied and ventriloquized post-individuality, one functionally appropriate to mass culture and mass society, and reducing the need for overt violence in the maintenance of a regime of social control.

Adorno's observation of the mechanics of the culture industry in the prosperous United States grounded his suspicion that the fully realized form of that totally administered society would be, unlike European fascism, efficient, subtle, predominantly if not consistently peaceful, and largely sublimated, exerting control simultaneously at the level of institutions and of personality structures. The description of a *generally* nonviolent domination had significant qualifications. In Tocqueville's case, the discussion centered on the facts of slavery and the extermination of

America's Native American population. In the case of the authoritarian or anti-Semitic personality, the diagnosis was not to be confined to the form of mind necessary for the success of authoritarian rule, since the Institute of Social Research theorists understood fascism to occupy one relatively unstable end of a spectrum of modern mass society, whose more stable center they saw embodied in the postwar triumph of a distinctively American form of administration. This is why Adorno also focuses on the physiognomy of a highly complex and moderately efficient bureaucratic mechanism, administering an ever-increasing share of citizen's private mental lives, twinned with a consumption-based market economy that had learned through social-scientific methods to generate continuous consumer anxieties and fantasies for the unending creation of new needs.

This crystallized in the form of a culture industry designed for the provision of mass distraction, which Leo Löwenthal famously described as "psychoanalysis in reverse," and the emptying of the spheres of voluntary associations in civil society, supplanted by seamless administration of formerly political issues as technical problems, and the production of substitute satisfactions to fill the gaps in ego structures previously sustained through communal action, political agency, and social solidarity.

In the midst of the American half century of middle-class triumphalism following the war, Adorno was vividly aware of his status as a remnant of the ebbing world of high bourgeois European culture, even if that had already aged into senescence by the time of Adorno's own youth. This self-understanding is both biographical and beyond biography at one and the same time: an outsider status as ambassador and caretaker of a world in decline. As Tocqueville to aristocracy, so Adorno to the era of the high bourgeoisie—lateness entails a mode of thinking, feeling, and judging from an epistemic standpoint out of joint and, simultaneously, refiguring the experience of world loss as a bittersweet insight into the smaller, colorless world replacing it. *Minima Moralia* chronicles the last days of the high culture of the European bourgeoisie and the world it built, from the point of view of a late member observing, simultaneously, the rise of mass culture, in its American commercialist and its German fascist variants. In pointillist style, the book's entries move back and forth between finely observed details of autobiography, individual moments of horror arising from the descent of the European bourgeoisie into fascism, and fragments and snippets of literature and poetry.

The work's deliberate conflation of genres includes a parodic evocation of the gentleman's guide to proper manners and comportment in the bourgeois interior: the vanishing parlors, drawing rooms, concert halls, and galleries of the European nineteenth century. While Tocqueville was still able to draw on the fading tradition of aristocratic elegance and courtesy (including elegance of thinking), *Minima Moralia* can be read as an extended reflection not only on the loss of the possibility of an upright and moral existence—morality being among the great inventions of the nineteenth-century European middle classes—but on the loss of the possibility of a well-mannered tasteful life, a life of middle-class culture. In *Minima Moralia* and elsewhere, Adorno chooses to see himself as a specter, having outlived the death of the European bourgeoisie.[25]

For this reason, *Minima Moralia* is also a sustained exercise in condescension and snobbery.[26] From the perspective of the last bourgeois, the new mass human being is not just suffering new modes of domination. It is also spectacularly annoying. Post-bourgeois humanity is twitchy—it can no longer sit patiently and attentively through a musical performance. It has lost the ability to open and close a door quietly. It has lost the ability to travel, to visit, to host a visitor ("Chilly Hospitality," 116; "Auction," 119). In a direct echo of Tocqueville's startled reaction to American frenetic busyness, Adorno complains that "the haste, nervousness, restlessness observed since the rise of the big cities is now spreading in the manner of an epidemic, as did once the plague and cholera. In the process forces are being unleashed that were undreamed of by the scurrying passer-by of the nineteenth century. Everybody must have projects all the time. The maximum must be extracted from leisure" (139). The use of powerful devices like cars generates a peculiar bodily comportment where lulling leisure melds with the constant potential for mechanical violence.[27]

Even tact—that preeminent virtue of the European bourgeoisie, the capacity to turn egalitarian tolerance into something elevated—for all its admixture of intimacy and alienation, vanishes from the world along with the bourgeois individual. The latter, as Tocqueville described, had liquidated all "forms of hierarchical respect" (36), conventional rules regulating the interaction of persons and bodies. Cast into the post-traditional landscape of social equality, and separated from the majority of their fellow human beings by mere economic privilege, democratic individuals required more than purely political virtues. Tact had allowed isolated, "Cartesian" individuals to accommodate one another without explicit customary rules grounded in traditional social distinctions. It made possible the distinctiveness of bourgeois private life, into which Tocqueville's individuals were so eager to retreat, abandoning the political public sphere. Now even that, Adorno writes, is gone. The cluelessness of modern subjects, their alternation between indifference and nosiness, their haplessness in dealing with tacit rules for acknowledging the other, is still more small-format evidence for the waning capacity to make reflective judgments about particulars, above all particular other people. Tact had required a form of humaneness, not without its contradictions, that was specific to the historical hour of the bourgeoisie. A kind of distinctly American, paid-to-be-here obligatory corporate sunniness was replacing it. Tact had required the "discrimination of differences" (37), which mass culture was in the process of liquidating. It was being turned into a mere tactic.[28]

The bourgeois individual, whose advent Tocqueville diagnosed as ultimately incompatible with the forms of associational life and habits of mind in the exercise of political freedom, had itself run its course and was in the process of liquidation through new technologies of obliteration that fascism had found so important, but also liquidation through the "mild" encroachment of mass culture, corporate control, and anonymous power. Under these, the bourgeois institution of individuality lives on as a hollow form, a ghost of itself. Adorno cannot mourn its fading with any real enthusiasm, any more than Tocqueville could seriously long for the lost sweetness of the *ancien régime*. Yet like Tocqueville, Adorno sees the process of loss—including the loss of the social basis of his own subjectivity—as offering at least a degree of clarity regarding what replaces it. For what occupies the place of individuality is a new mode of stupidity—a characteristic admixture of irrationality, incapacity and disinclination for sustained thinking, emotional lability, and susceptibility to political dogmas—that fascism and postdemocratic America, for Adorno, largely share.[29]

There is a direct link, in other words, between the loss of bourgeois virtues, ambivalent though they were, and the advent of a neo-stupid mode of living adapted to prevailing conditions. It is at this point that the hyperconscious elitism of *Minima Moralia* comes into its own as a core element of Adorno's late epistemology. That epistemology conceives of experienced truth in terms of the awareness of its encroaching disappearance from the political and social worlds, in the face of an economic world that never needed it and has indeed become, in many ways, hostile to it. Like the subjective capacity for a full or undistorted form of experience, the epistemic capacity for discursive truth *via* conceptual connection or synthesis—judgment—has been exiled from any social role, living on spectrally as a kind of negative space or the awareness of a loss. The advent of post-truth is a phenomenon of both structure and unit, of the decay of subjective capacities for discernment and "the objectively determined decay of logical evidence as such." The collapse of the very social foundations for true statements and the advent of the post-truth world seemed to Adorno, seventy years ago, as elements of a crisis, but visible only on premises that affirm once again the kind of epistemic elitism, late epistemology, that Adorno could neither escape nor in good conscience endorse.

"Things have come to a pass," Adorno writes,

> where lying sounds like truth, truth like lying. Each statement, each piece of news, each thought has been pre-formed by the centers of the culture industry. Whatever lacks the familiar trace of such pre-formation lacks credibility, the more so because the institutions of public opinion accompany what they send for by a thousand factual proofs and all the plausibility that total power can lay hands on. Truth that opposes these pressures not only appears improbable, but is in addition too feeble to make any headway in competition with their highly concentrated machinery of dissemination. (108)

The demand for truth in the midst of the culture industry's output is unfulfillable but not futile, as it at least helps strip away the quasi-natural appearance of that output and render it visible as what it is. In a culture determined to abandon the category of truth, calling out lies is drudgery compared to what might have been the joy of thinking. And into this post-truth world steps the post-individual, a category central to Adorno's diagnosis of the conjunction of capitalism and neoliberal democratic mass society, but one that here we can register only in its moment of contact with Tocqueville's late-republican lament for the loss of associational life.

At the core of Adorno's late modern lament is the rise of post-individuality as an outsourcing to administration (an "immense tutelary power") of the last vestiges of a form of subjectivity capable of experience and thought. Experience and thought, institutionalized, were what Adorno clung to as the exemplary accomplishment of the bourgeoisie: culture. And even where his American sojourn gave him grudging admiration for forms of mass democracy, the country's apparent capacity to do largely without culture was not only distasteful to the homeless dilettante. It was part of the larger process where subjectivity lost its inner power of resistance to the psychic pressures leading from fugitive forms of political freedom to a leveled-out authoritarian future where the hollow idols of bourgeois individuals stumbled across a landscape of "mild" despotism.

Adorno describes the modern, late, postdemocratic individual as a kind of postsubject of this kind. As an exemplary institution of bourgeois modernity, individuality promised uniqueness but delivered a reversion back to its other, to sameness and repetition, to myth. The liquidation of the individual in mass culture does hollow out the institution of individuality, but it does not liquidate it fully; the postindividul is not the same as the nonindividual. Administration makes intelligent use of this hollowed form: "The disaster," Adorno says, "does not take the form of a radical elimination of what existed previously; rather the things that history has condemned are dragged along dead, neutralized and impotent as ignominious ballast" (133). Without this zombie form of individuality persisting into the present, without the expectation of the distinctiveness of a particular human life remaining on constant offer, mass society could not succeed in exerting such enormous pressure for persons to produce and consume at levels commensurate with its endless requirements.[30]

If this prognostication has any practical purpose—holding off or forestalling, or at least slowing, the fading of a form of democratic political life—then the irony is that it is justified through a form of radical critique entirely dependent on the repurposing of elitism, by which I simply mean the claim, implicit or otherwise, that the critic's insights arise from capacities associated with a formerly dominant social group.

It is this elitism that Adorno is probably most closely associated with, though I hope the description here of late epistemology might complicate that standard criticism somewhat. Adorno's analyses of the psychic work of mass-cultural commodities such as television or jazz can be taken in a sense that is also possibly Tocquevillian—as small tactics in a broader strategy attempting to insert certain forms of subjective braces into an ever-narrowing space where democratic civil society makes contact with the exercise of democratic popular sovereignty. This point, insofar as it is it has any validity, may also help to answer an otherwise puzzling aspect of Adorno's work as a social critic: offering the bleakest possible diagnosis of American style administered society in the 1940s, while at the same time participating with full enthusiasm on his return to West Germany in the 1950s, through mass media, to promote new forms of democratic pedagogy.[31]

On his return to Germany, Adorno placed considerable hope in the possibility that intermediate institutions within a withered but surviving civil society would continue to impede total administration, and could under favorable conditions continue to transmit, as Habermas put it, opinion and will formation from a democratic public sphere to the institutionalized level of parliamentary bodies. He did this despite a profoundly antirepublican cast of mind that marks one of his many dissimilarities to Tocqueville.[32]

Tocqueville, the last aristocrat and the ambivalent democrat, made a notably poor democratic politician in his brief and unfortunate foray into national politics. Adorno, the last bourgeois and the elitist snob, culture vulture and ruthless critic of every aspect of contemporary mass culture, in many respects was a rather good political actor, if we extend (as we should) the conception of political activity to include the kind of interventions into the nascent political public culture of post-catastrophe West Germany that Adorno saw himself as duty-bound to engage in. These he carried out with measurable success, nudging the process of German democratization in a direction that was more self-critical, less tolerant of the old style of nationalist sewage, than many had predicted and feared.

There is of course an irreducible element of elitism and condescension in the invocation of grand Kantian ambitions such as a public education *"nach Mündigkeit."*[33] Even (or especially) the immature and psychologically underdeveloped will not appreciate their fellow citizen, the elite political theorist, thinking of them in this way. They are correct in their suspicion of our scorn, and right to resent it. But Adorno was not suggesting that the grand cultural tradition of German philosophical idealism could save secondary school children from susceptibility to authoritarianism. He thought that what children needed was not more *Geist* but more psychic and social space to develop a degree of healthy skepticism and the habits of self-reflexivity before they were engulfed by accommodation and adaptation, which invariably demand that one think and feel less and less, and rely more and more on the "tutelary power" to assume responsibility for one's own subjective life. "Education" for Adorno meant, not least, protection accorded to persons for the development of sufficient ego strength (*Ich-stärke*) to mount more effective and durable resistance to that tutelary power—to take a more substantive part in their own social mediation. This suggests that thinking is less a cognitive operation than a comportment, a way of living, with a strong affective dimension, since among other things it will forseeably render the process of adaptation and integration into prevailing social norms and institutions more difficult—and rightly so.

Evoking "sufficient ego strength" also risks merely reproducing the frozen negation of the "authoritarian personality." But dialectical thinking—and that is ultimately what "late epistemology" means—is precisely the subjective capacity to resist the temptation of permitting concepts, which are dynamic and protean, to stop at the point most pleasing to the thinking subject. Late epistemology can at least in principle be refashioned so that it appears less like the condescending scorn of a fading cultural mandarinate, and more like the outline of a pedagogy of resistance. Theory has its practical moment in the demand for a new kind of democratic pedagogy. "Maturity" entails, among other things, the capacity to see the particular *through* the totality. Adorno's claim is that this kind of thinking is in effect a psychic bulwark against authoritarianism, since it operates as a dam against the social demands of the whole suite of epistemic short-cuts that a neoliberal capitalist social world foists on its subjects.

For Adorno, "thinking" itself is the quintessential form of active resistance to the hegemony of mass society and its internal dynamic leading to quiescence and authoritarian rule.[34] "Thinking"—and here no sharper contrast to Heidegger is possible—is the capacity to employ concepts, to make judgments, dialectically. This requires a degree of self-reflexivity, the capacity to think while also reflecting continuously on the relation between one's subjective thinking and the social totality in which one's subjectivity, like one's available concepts, are mediated through the objective conditions in which one thinks them. This fact endows dialectics with its odd, distaff, and oblique connection to social hope, since on its own terms, there is really no possibility of a "type" of postdemocratic subjectivity that could ever qualify as something natural, fixed, or inevitable. Authoritarians are stupid. But if stupidity is at heart a social and not a natural category, it is just as malleable, contingent, and susceptible to democratic hope as any other. Stupidity in this socially constructed sense is not just compatible with education but implies it.

And what of us? As we face a wave of antidemocratic political change that is at once unprecedented and wearily familiar, it's tempting to say that we, producers and consumers of political theory, are all late epistemologists now, insofar as we continue to practice theory-making at all.

But our standard assumptions regarding the origins and dynamics of popular political movements may fatally underestimate the degree to which the same dynamics of neoliberal capitalism have successfully harnessed globalized media technologies, cultural symbologies, and public spaces in ways that render even nativist reactions to neoliberal globalization compatible with—even a piece of—the economic imperatives that now drive the pace and direction of global politics in a way unprecedented in human history. Perhaps the parsimonious explanation for authoritarianism is that neoliberal global capitalism is finally prepared to take the momentous step of shaking itself free of its long historical association with democratic self-rule. If that is true, then the suspiciously uniform affective array that mobilizes electorates to vote themselves into authoritarianism—resentment, fear, and rage—may be easier to explain as functional imperatives of an emergent system of mild global economic governance, which doesn't so much accommodate itself to extreme affects on the part of its clients as make use of them for its own purposes.

Yet this also suggests that the late critiques Tocqueville and Adorno proffered at either end, so to speak, of this historical epoch remain indispensable resources—despite their tendency to reduce the theorists' fellow citizens to the status of animals (sheep) or children. Sensing the steady encroachment of systemic imperatives as replacements of the native capacity for critical reflective thought need not take this additional step. One of the great virtues of dialectical thinking is just this: performed consistently, it undermines the temptation to lay down the burden of thinking through one's own commitments.

If this hard work renders socially engineered stupidity even marginally less prevalent, it is work worth doing. As a component of an enlarged methodological stance designed to comprehend and interpret the subjective dimension of authoritarianism in ways that current social science seems unable to do, it may be the, or at least a, democratic moment within political theory—that might help not just interpret, but change, what seems to be an impending authoritarian world.

NOTES

For helpful and instructive comments and criticisms I am very grateful to audiences at Pennsylvania State University, the Czech Academy of Social Sciences, and the Philosophy Department at the University of Essex, in particular Amy Allen, Timo Jütten, Fabian

Freyenhagen, James Ingram, Rainer Forst, Robin Celikates, Peter Gordon, and Bill Scheuerman; and to two anonymous reviewers for the University of Chicago Press.

1. Constitutional retrogression is defined as "incremental (but ultimately substantial) decay in three basic predicates of democracy—competitive elections, liberal rights to speech and association, and the adjudicative and administrative rule of law necessary for democratic choice to thrive," in Aziz Z. Huq and Tom Ginzburg, "How to Lose a Constitutional Democracy," *UCLA Law Review* 65 (2018): 6. On disconnection, see Roberto Stefan Foa and Yascha Mounk, "The Democratic Disconnect." *Journal of Democracy* 27, no. 3 (July 2016): 5–17.

2. For a comprehensive recent account of "latent" authoritarianism as a suite of subjective attitudes and affects, see Karen Stenner, *The Authoritarian Dynamic* (Cambridge: Cambridge University Press, 2005).

3. Georg Lukacs, *Theory of the Novel* (Cambridge: MIT Press, 1971), 22.

4. For a lucid reconstruction and comparison of Tocqueville and Adorno as observers of American democracy, see Claus Offe, *Reflections on America: Tocqueville, Weber and Adorno in the United States* (Cambridge: Polity Press, 2005). The best single account in English of Adorno's American experiences is David Jenemann, *Adorno in America* (Minneapolis: University of Minnesota Press, 2007). See also Thomas Wheatland, *The Frankfurt School in Exile* (Minneapolis: University of Minnesota Press, 2009).

5. Again, see Jenemann, *Adorno in America*.

6. Offe, *Reflections on America*, 4–6.

7. Alexis de Tocqueville, *Democracy in America*, ed. and trans. Harvey C. Mansfield and Delba Winthrop (Chicago: University of Chicago Press, 2000). Subsequent references will be indicated by page numbers in parentheses.

8. Hannah Arendt, *The Origins of Totalitarianism* (New York: Schocken, 2004).

9. Patrick J. Dineen, *Why Liberalism Failed* (New Haven, CT: Yale University Press, 2018), 75ff.

10. See Melvin Richter, "Tocqueville on Threats to Liberty in Democracies," in *The Cambridge Companion to Tocqueville*, ed. Cheryl B. Welch (Cambridge: Cambridge University Press, 2006), 245–75.

11. Immanuel Kant, "The Contest of the Faculties: A Renewed Attempt to Answer the Question: 'Is the Human Race Continually Improving?,'" in Hans Reiss, editor, *Kant's Political Writings* (Cambridge: Cambridge University Press, 1970), 185.

12. See Tocqueville, *Democracy in America*, 411 ff.

13. As Tocqueville puts it, "Aristocracy naturally leads the mind to contemplation of the past and settles it there. Democracy, by contrast, gives men a kind of distinctive disgust for the old" (382).

14. Sheldon Wolin, *Tocqueville between Two Worlds: The Making of a Political and Theoretical Life* (Princeton, NJ: Princeton University Press, 2001), 88.

15. On the distinctive democratic (and American) distaste for time, Tocqueville writes, "Among aristocratic nations, as families remain for centuries in the same condition, often on the same spot, all generations become, as it were, contemporaneous. A man almost always knows his forefathers and respects them; he thinks he already sees his remote descendants and he loves them. He willingly imposes duties on himself toward the former and the latter, and he will frequently sacrifice his personal gratifications to those who went before and to those who will come after him.... Among democratic nations new families are constantly springing up, others are constantly falling away, and all that remain change their condition; the web of time is every instant broken and the track of generations effaced. Those who went before are soon forgotten; of those who will come after, no one has any idea: the interest of man is confined to those in close propinquity to himself.... Thus not only does democracy make every man forget his ancestors, but it hides his descendants and separates his contemporaries from him: it throws him back forever upon himself alone and threatens in the end to confine him entirely within the solitude of his own heart" (466).

16. As Wolin puts it, "As an element in a theoretical strategy, archaism aims at unsettling the present, bringing it to a temporary pause, insisting that it historicize its self-understanding. But the present instinctively resists historicization. It wants nothing more than to interpret itself by itself, that is, by its own notions and categories, by its own self-confirming narrative. The intrusion forces the present out of its self-contained hermeneutical circle. Archaism can accomplish this effect because, unlike the present, it has been stripped of its context. It confronts the present like some displaced refugee caught between times and without place. Precisely because it cannot represent the abandoned past to a present whose identity is staked on the death of the past, the archaic trails an odor of death, an unwelcome reminder to the present that change not only brings new things into the world but causes other things to languish and disappear. The archaic forces the modern into self-questioning, slowing the urge to totalize." Wolin, *Tocqueville between Two Worlds*, 566. Offe makes the comparison to Benjamin's dialectical images explicit; see Offe, *Reflections on America*, 9–10n13.

17. As Melvin Richter puts it, what Tocqueville has in mind is a form of domination "not as exercised by an intolerant majority denying the freedom to form and express opinions, but by a beneficent centralized state apparatus satisfying all the needs of its subjects who are represented as atomized individuals or families concerned only with their own material well-being. The regime ruling them would be at once absolute, omnipresent, regular in its procedures, detailed in their application, paternal in its anticipation of all its subjects' wants, and nonviolent, even mild." Richter, "Tocqueville on Threats," 255.

18. On Tocqueville and technology, see Benjamin Storey, "Tocqueville on Technology, *New Atlantis*, no. 40 (Fall 2013), 48–71.

19. On Tocqueville's ambivalent attitude toward the role of the intermediate institutions of democratic civil society, see Dana Villa, "Tocqueville and Civil Society," in *Cambridge Companion to Tocqueville*.

20. "I see an innumerable crowd of like and equal men who revolve on themselves without repose, procuring the small and vulgar pleasures with which they fill their souls. Each of them, withdrawn and apart, is like a stranger to the destiny of all the others: his children and his particular friends form the whole of the human species for him; as for dwelling with his fellow citizens, he is beside them, but he does not see them; he touches them and does not feel them; he exists only in himself and for himself alone and if a family still remains for him, one can at least say that he no longer has a native country" (663).

21. For an interesting discussion of this point, see Jason Frank, *The Democratic Sublime: Aesthetics and Assembly in the Age of Revolution* (Oxford: Oxford University Press, 2018).

22. There are obvious connections, which I cannot explore here, to what Marcuse would describe as the mechanism of repressive desublimation. See Herbert Marcuse, *One-Dimensional Man: Studies in the Ideology of Advanced Industrial Society* (Boston: Beacon Press, 1993), 78ff.

23. See the informative discussion in Cheryl B. Welch, *De Tocqueville* (Oxford: Oxford University Press, 2001), 245ff.

24. Theodor W. Adorno, *Minima Moralia. Reflections from Damaged Life* (London: Verso, 1974), 106. All further references indicated by parenthetical page numbers.

25. For an excellent treatment of this fascinating topic, see Asaf Angermann, "The Ghosts of Normativity: Temporality and Recurrence in Adorno's Ethics of Dissonance," *Germanic Review: Literature, Culture, Theory* 90, no. 4 (2015): 260–72.

26. On Adorno's distinctive affect as a European mandarin in his interactions with Americans, see in particular David E. Morrison, "*Kultur* and Culture: The Case of Theodor W. Adorno and Paul F. Lazarsfeld," *Social Research* 45, no. 2 (Summer 1978): 331–55, and Martin Jay, *Permanent Exiles: Essays on the Intellectual Migration from Germany to America* (New York: Columbia University Press, 1986), chap. 9, "Adorno in America."

27. "Which driver is not tempted, merely by the power of his en-

gine, to wipe out the vermin of the street, pedestrians, children and cyclists? The movements machines demand of their users already have the violent, hard-hitting jerkiness of Fascist maltreatment" (40).

28. For an illuminating treatment of this topic, see J. M. Bernstein, *Adorno: Disenchantment and Ethics* (Cambridge: Cambridge University Press, 2001), 64–68.

29. See Adorno's remarkable backhanded compliment to America, to the effect that his American years had done him the unexpected favor of permitting him, for the first time, to "see culture from the outside." "Scientific Experiences of a European Scholar in America," in *Critical Models: Interventions and Catchwords* (New York: Columbia University Press, 1998), 239.

30. Dana Villa has described this dummy or pseudo-individuality that Adorno diagnoses as "a condition where virtually everything we do is, at some level, an imitation of the looks, attitudes and behavioral types we have previously encountered in advertising and mass media. In such a world—a world of pervasive, unrestrained, and often unconscious mimesis—the peculiarity of the self (that is, what we take to be a marker of 'genuine' individuality) turns out to be, in fact, a 'socially conditioned monopoly commodity misrepresented as natural.'" Villa, *Public Freedom* (Princeton, NJ: Princeton University Press, 2008), 149. Villa also sees in this regard the connection between Adorno's and Tocqueville's diagnoses of a peculiarly American form of post-individuality grounded in the leveling effect of material cravings (156ff).

31. On Adorno's postwar political views and their relation to the radical critique of the totally administered society, see the comprehensive discussion in Alex Demirovic, *Der nonkonformistische Intellektuelle. Die Entwicklung der Kritischen Theorie zur Frankfurter Schule* (Frankfurt: Suhrkamp, 1999). For a critical discussion, see Max Pensky, "Beyond the Message in a Bottle: The Other Critical Theory," *Constellations* 10, no. 1 (March 2003): 135–44. For a recent excellent discussion, see also Fabian Freyenhagen, "Adorno's Politics: Theory and Praxis in Germany's 1960s," *Philosophy and Social*

Criticism 40, no. 9 (2014): 867–93. See also Shannon Mariotti,
Adorno and Democracy: The American Years (Lexington: University of
Kentucky Press, 2016).

32. I thank Bill Scheuerman for reminding me of this.

33. See Theodor W. Adorno and Hellmut Becker, "Education for
Maturity and Responsibility," *History of the Human Sciences* 12, no. 3
(1999): 21–34.

34. See Adorno, "Resignation," in *Critical Models*, 293.